MARTHA STEWART'S
Hors d'Oeuvres

*The Creation and Presentation
of Fabulous Finger Foods*

Photographs by Peter Bosch

Designed by Vincent Winter

Recipes and Styling with Sara Foster

Clarkson N. Potter, Inc./Publishers NEW YORK
DISTRIBUTED BY CROWN PUBLISHERS, INC.

Published by Clarkson N. Potter, Inc., 225 Park Avenue South, New York, New York 10003 and represented in Canada by the Canadian MANDA Group Manufactured in Japan

Photographs on pages 74 (left), 76 (right), and 78–79, 79 (top) © 1983 by Jerry Simpson. Photograph on page 128 by Andrew Stewart. Photograph on page 78 (top) © 1983 by Joseph Kugielsky.

Library of Congress Cataloging-in-Publication Data
Stewart, Martha.
   Hors d'oeuvres: the creation and presentation of fabulous finger foods.

   Includes index.
   1. Cookery (Appetizers)
   I. Title.
TX740.S74   1984   641.8'12
     84-11591
ISBN 0-517-55455-0

10 9 8 7

TO MY EDITOR

CAROLYN HART GAVIN

with LOVE and DEEP APPRECIATION

Contents

ACKNOWLEDGMENTS   ix
INTRODUCTION   1

CHAPTER ONE
Tea Party in the Library
Page   17

CHAPTER TWO
Christmas Cocktails
Page   27

CHAPTER THREE
Country Kitchen Hors d'Oeuvres
Page   34

CHAPTER FOUR
The Outdoor Barbecue
Page   47

CHAPTER FIVE
Champagne and Valentines
Page   57

CHAPTER SIX
A Spring Wedding Reception
Page   69

CHAPTER SEVEN
Oriental Cocktails in the Parlor
Page   81

CHAPTER EIGHT

Seafood at the Beach

Page 91

CHAPTER NINE

The Grand and Elegant Party

Page 101

CHAPTER TEN

Antipasto Party in the Kitchen

Page 108

CHAPTER ELEVEN

The Breakfast Buffet

Page 121

CHAPTER TWELVE

Tex-Mex Hors d'Oeuvres

Page 127

CHAPTER THIRTEEN

Fancy Cocktails

Page 139

CHAPTER FOURTEEN

Master Recipes

Page 149

→≫≪←

INDEX

Page 160

Acknowledgments

THERE ARE MANY PEOPLE I WOULD LIKE TO THANK FOR THEIR HELP, INSPIRATION, AND SUPPORT IN THE CREATION OF THIS, MY THIRD BOOK.

To my friends at Clarkson Potter and Crown for their constant good will and continuing interest in all my projects: Nat Wartels, Alan Mirken, Bruce Harris, Carol Southern, Michael Fragnito, Carolyn Hart Gavin, Kathy Powell, Gael Dillon, Lynne Arany, Susan Eilertsen, Sally Berk, Michelle Sidrane, Phyllis Fleiss, Jo Fagan, Rusty Porter, Ed Otto, and Laurie Stark.

To Sara Foster, who worked for me as catering chef for two years, for her assistance in the creation of new recipes and variations of old recipes for this book and for helping to style many of the photographs.

To Peter Bosch for his exquisite photography. To his assistant Roch Craford, for his energetic and expert help.

To the members of my kitchen staff, especially Susan Ward for her careful styling and fashioning of finger foods, Jane Stacey, Marsha Harris, Robyn Fairclough, and Edna de Souza.

To Necy Fernandes for her extraordinary help in keeping home, kitchens, and parties organized.

To Marinda Freeman and Wendy Bartlett for running the office and managing our complicated schedules so competently and pleasantly.

To Rafael Rosario for his wild-rice pancakes recipe and for his managing of our wonderful New York party staff.

To my brother George Christiansen and his wife, Rita, for the use of their cobalt blue glassware. To my sister Laura Herbert for the loan of all the wonderful pink Depression glass. To my sister Kathy Evans for her help in creating the delightful cocktail party and for the use of her colorful, beautiful weavings.

To my friends Lynne and Wayne Rogers, Susan and Tony Victoria, Ruth and Paul Leserman, Ruth and Gil Kraft, Donna and Henry Clarke, Jr., who so generously permitted us the use of their homes for photography.

To my very special friends, both private and corporate, who have eaten and, I think, enjoyed so many of the hors d'oeuvres described in this book.

To Michael Skott for another lovely jacket photograph.

To Vincent Winter for his superb and clear design.

To my husband, Andy, for his continuing appetite, and to my daughter Alexis for her ongoing critiques.

Introduction

My husband, Andy, and I gave our first cocktail party eighteen years ago when we were living in one of those spacious, high-ceilinged, rent-controlled apartments on Riverside Drive in New York. The windows of the apartment overlooked Riverside Park and the Hudson River, and if you craned your neck you could see the George Washington Bridge. At night the view was especially beautiful—we could see the lights on the Jersey side of the river, the occasional boat on the dark water, and, in the foreground, the large treetops of the park.

This was a Christmas open house, and we invited absolutely everyone we knew. I had lots of time in those days, since I was at home on maternity leave from my job. I spent many happy weeks planning and preparing for that party, with our three-month-old daughter Alexis watching and "helping" from her baby chair in the kitchen.

. . . .

Shining copper trays are so beautiful, especially when garnished with ivy and spring blossoms.

1

A silver tray is lined with curly parsley and galax leaves and decorated with freesia. Fresh dill in the footed silver dish makes a wonderful bed for hors d'oeuvres. Ivy, white lilacs, carnations, and lemon leaves decorate the other trays.

. . . .

I had grown up in a large family, and so preparing quantities of food for many people never frightened me. The menu for this party was as lavish and varied as we could afford. Even then, I believed that one should offer the very best to one's guests and never skimp. I baked a big country ham and Polish sausages, mounds of biscuits and muffins, and bite-size quiches filled with spinach and chicken. We splurged on oysters from our local fishmonger (in those days they were only fifteen cents each) and the best cheese we could find, including the new rage of New York—French Brie! We served inexpensive French table wine and champagne and a new version of eggnog Andy and I invented on the spot made with bourbon and cognac (it has since become a family favorite).

I started baking fruitcakes, pound cakes, and plum pudding two weeks before the party. A little seven-year-old neighbor named Claire came every day after school to help me chop and cut up fruit. We also made all kinds of Christmas cookies—pressed butter cookies, nut balls, and cutout cookies—with recipes that had been in my family for generations.

The week before the party Andy and I drove up to Vermont and cut lots of evergreen boughs, which we fashioned into wreaths and swags for the doorways and hallways of the apartment. The fragrance was incredible.

Somehow, everything came together at the party. The guests ate all the food on the table, drank gallons of eggnog, and sang Christmas carols until well past midnight. It was a memorable party and has become an annual tradition at our house. The location has changed since our family moved to Connecticut thirteen years ago, and the menus are different to keep up with my changing ideas about food. Now the ham is sliced very thin and wrapped around pencil asparagus; the quiches are filled with crabmeat, St. André cheese, and herbs; and the oysters are dressed with spinach and sun-dried tomatoes. But the feeling is the same as it was on Riverside Drive.

The cocktail party is still my favorite way to entertain groups of friends, as well as one of my favorite catering assignments. Hors d'oeuvres, I have discovered, can be almost any type of food, of any ethnic origin, prepared in bite-size tastes which can be picked up and held in the fingers or placed on small plates, until eaten. Hors d'oeuvres are generally savory (not sweet), served before a meal, as an accompaniment to drinks. Sometimes they are served as a substitute for a meal, in which case they are heartier and more plentiful. Less frequently they are a combination of savory and sweet offerings and do indeed constitute enough in the way of variety and quantity to replace a meal.

Shaker wood trays are lined with lemon leaves and curly parsley and radicchio; a vine basket with galax leaves and ivy.

. . . .

Above right: *Iced vodka, garnished with heather, hyacinths, and asparagus ferns, poured into an amethyst-stemmed goblet.* Above left: *Copper heart trays of different sizes decorated with tiny orchids and galax leaves, carnations, and ivy. The large tray holds a hollowed-out red cabbage for dip, a tiny Oriental eggplant, a black pepper, and radicchio.*

. . . .

Overleaf: *Rental glasses come in a marvelous array of shapes and sizes today. The ones pictured are all from one party-rental supplier.*

I love hors d'oeuvres because they provide an opportunity to be wonderfully creative in the kitchen. Variations can be almost endless. An old standby like melon and prosciutto can be deliciously transformed by wrapping wedges of green honeydew with black Japanese seaweed and inserting a large lump of crabmeat under the seaweed. Caviar and sour cream can be served on small, perfect leaves of Bibb lettuce instead of on toast or blini. A log of chevre can be served bathed in a lemony cream sauce and garnished with fresh chives and chive blossoms instead of with the more traditional oil and herbs. Large red and green seedless grapes, which for years we have been rolling in Roquefort cheese and chopped nuts, can be split and piped decoratively with softened triple crème cheese. The possibilities are endless.

Some of the recipes in this book will be familiar to readers of *Entertaining.* They are included because they are the most asked-for hors d'oeuvres in our repertoire, but I have added new variations. We are constantly experimenting and changing our hors d'oeuvres; rarely do we make exactly the same hors d'oeuvres twice. Recently, I catered a party for the Cooper-Hewitt Museum in which the food was designed to complement an exhibit of American Plains Indian art. When we

finalized the menu, I realized that only three hors d'oeuvres were ones I had done before. Fried sweet potato sticks, smoked duck on jalapeño cornbread muffins, pickled chiles, and deep-fried spicy chick peas were a few of the recipes we had created (which will have to be included in a future book!). Such is the nature of hors d'oeuvres, and one of the reasons I never tire of making them.

Another reason I love hors d'oeuvres is because they are so beautiful to look at. Hors d'oeuvres, made from the freshest, most impeccable ingredients, carefully prepared, and artistically presented, are like small jewels, perfect in every detail. A wilted garnish, wrinkled asparagus, or soggy cucumber slices have no place on an hors d'oeuvre tray. An unusual decoration, one perfect blossom, a bouquet of herbs, or a shiny leaf should serve to enhance the hors d'oeuvres, never to detract from their perfection. Each hors d'oeuvre should be as uniformly like all the others of its kind as possible. Only one kind of hors d'oeuvre should be arranged on a tray, this as much for aesthetics as for practicality. It is unfair to the guests to present them with a tray full of choices, some of which might need explanation, while they are engaged in conversations. It is much better to display them simply and beautifully.

Stuffed grape leaves, large purple grapes, and blueberries look very beautiful on amethyst glass. I love to collect all colored glass, but amethyst is my personal favorite, and I have a large collection of it gathered from all over.

. . . .

A well-equipped kitchen makes the preparation of hors d'oeuvres much, much simpler. The tools, for the most part, are not expensive. Many can be found in kitchen-supply shops and gourmet stores or ordered through mail-order catalogs. Harder-to-find items often turn up in odd places, so be on the lookout for them. I have even located some of my most valued tools in Europe and at garage sales. The following tools are the ones I have found to be invaluable during my years of making hors d'oeuvres. This is the optimum list; many tools are not essential, just very useful.

⇒⇒⇒ *Equipment* ⇐⇐⇐

Food processor
Blender
Electric hand mixer

Electric spice grinder
Food mill
Pepper mill

⇒⇒⇐⇐

Cutting and Slicing Tools

Sharp stainless steel knives in various sizes (Henckel's is one excellent brand I use)
Sharp Japanese paring knives
Long stainless steel semi-serrated knife for slicing gravlax and salmon (Henckel's Super-fection line)
Chinese cleaver for chopping
Sharp Japanese steel cleaver (more lightweight and smaller than Chinese cleavers)

Knife steel for sharpening
Mandoline or small slicer
Pizza cutter
Pastry wheel
Metal pastry scraper
Biscuit cutters: 1", $1\frac{1}{2}$", and 2" hearts; 1", $1\frac{1}{4}$", $1\frac{1}{2}$", and $2\frac{1}{4}$" fluted and plain rounds; 2" and $2\frac{1}{4}$" ovals

⇒⇒⇐⇐

Pans and Containers

Assortment of tiny quiche and tartlet pans
Pain de mie pan
Porcelain coeur à la crème mold
Flat metal baking sheets (stainless or tin-lined)
Cooling racks
Colanders for draining vegetables
Japanese metal strainers on bamboo handles

3", 6", and 8" strainers for sifting flour and sugar and straining sauces
Large portable bread board
Measuring spoons and cups
1 pint, 1 quart, and 1 gallon covered plastic containers for storage of dips and frozen hors d'oeuvres
Styrofoam or insulated coolers for transport or storage

—>>》《《—

Miscellaneous Kitchen Equipment

10", 12", and 14" nylon pastry bags with various tips—some of my favorites are Ateco numbers 113, 123, 230, OB, 5B, BU8 (large tips), 2, 10, 12, 17, 47, 48, 86, 95, and 112 (small tips)—plus several sets of plastic adapters for the small tips

1", 2", and 4" high-quality brushes for applying glazes and brushing excess flour from pastry during rolling

Cooking spatulas in various sizes

Small metal spreading spatulas

Rubber spatulas

Rolling pin

Wire whisks of various sizes

Tongs in various sizes

Tweezers or needle nose pliers (available at hardware stores) for removing bones from fish, especially gravlax and smoked salmon

Small, flat hand grater

Sharp vegetable peeler

Mortar and pestle for making herb or garlic paste

Garlic press

Apple corer

Lemon zester

Paper frills

Parchment paper

Cheesecloth

Bamboo skewers of various lengths

—>>》《《—

Serving Equipment and Trays

Assorted silver, copper, brass, or lacquer trays

Assorted flat and handled baskets

Footed or stemmed platters

Odd serving dishes

Small bowls, molds, and wooden boxes

Collections of glassware for drinks

Linen and service napkins

Ribbons

Doilies

Decorative toothpicks and picks

—>>》《《—

Bar Equipment

Corkscrews

Can and bottle openers

Drink stirrers and swizzle sticks

Ice tub, ice chest, ice bucket

Jigger measures

Silent butler

Lemon zester

Small, sharp stainless steel knives

Large purple and green grapes, split and piped with triple crème cheese, and apple slices spread with softened chevre are arranged on cobalt blue glassware. A bouquet of sweet williams, delphinium, and hot pink stock accent the beautiful deep color of the plates and goblets.

. . . .

The hors d'oeuvres party is a versatile form of entertaining. As an informal get-together for friends, it is one of the easiest ways to entertain at home. Light hors d'oeuvres, either passed on trays or arranged on a buffet, can be served for two to three hours with assorted drinks. The number of hors d'oeuvres served should vary according to the time of the party. If it is a before-dinner reception, then the food can be light and tempting. If the party is "just cocktails," given later than the guests' usual dinnertime, the foods must be more substantial. An antipasto party, an outdoor barbecue, or a Tex-Mex buffet are some of the suggestions in this book for heartier fare.

The at-home wedding reception is another favorite time to

serve hors d'oeuvres only. Again, the timing must be appropriate, and if the reception is at mealtime, then the offerings must be numerous enough in quantity and variety to be considered a meal. Plan this type of reception for late afternoon, between 3 P.M. and 6 P.M., if hors d'oeuvres only are to be served.

One of the real advantages of an hors d'oeuvres party is that large numbers of guests can be easily accommodated. For the hostess, an hors d'oeuvres party is much less nerve-racking than a sit-down meal, more interesting, and more fun. Local fund raisers, gallery openings, holiday celebrations, and festive family occasions are all excellent reasons to entertain with cocktails and finger foods.

I have not included a crudité party in this book because the subject of crudité was so thoroughly covered in *Entertaining*, but there is an antipasto party that illustrates the same kind of colorful visual display. The crudité parties we are doing these days for our clients have gone through fundamental evolutionary changes, and we are using more and more tender baby vegetables—baby beets; turnips; zucchini; yellow squash; red, yellow, or blue potatoes; pearl onions; pencil asparagus; haricots verts; leeks; carrots; and sugar snap peas. These are combined with bite-size pieces of green or purple broccoli, white or purple cauliflower, broad beans, string beans, and snow peas—all of which must of course be blanched or steamed to tenderize and make them most appealing.

The visual appeal of any hors d'oeuvre is crucial to its success. Over the years, my style of decoration and garnishing has expanded to include the use of vegetables and herbs as well as flowers, ferns, leaves, lace, and ribbons. My assistants and I find that the time we spend garnishing a tray of hors d'oeuvres is often as important as the time spent on the actual making of them. An ungarnished tray somehow looks very unfinished when placed next to a tray on which we have arranged a spray of blossoms, or a mixed handful of herbs. Even the most ordinary of trays, from the silver-plated rental platters we often must use at large formal receptions to the flat round basket trays any of us own and use at home, always looks more intriguing and complete when we add some sort of garnish or covering. We have started to use what we call the "posy"—a bouquet of flowers, herbs, or leaves which is tied with a length of satin ribbon—laid on a tray next to the hors d'oeuvres. This is an amazingly simple way to decorate, for the posy can be used again and again on trays all during the party. For large parties we will make enough of these

Crudité is always popular with guests. Here, a melange of colorful bite-size vegetables makes a spectacular display.

· · · · · · · · · · · ·

Left: *Oriental spring rolls, little dumplings (called "potstickers"), and deep-fried zucchini blossoms are arranged on green Depression glass and Fire King plates, surrounded by green glass wine and water goblets, small sherry glasses, and compote cups. Bright yellow ranunculus flowers float in English ring containers.* Below: *Steamed haricots verts and courgettes with a lemony dipping sauce look especially appetizing on lovely cobalt blue glass.*

. . . .

European- and American-made colored glass is widely available in thrift shops and flea markets and is fun to collect. It also makes the presentation of hors d'oeuvres and drinks much more interesting.

. . . .

"bouquets" to garnish as many trays as there are varieties of hors d'oeuvres. As a tray is returned to be replenished, the posy is removed, the tray rinsed or cleaned, then refilled and the posy replaced.

I am always looking for new and different trays to use for the presentation of finger foods. As an alternative to silver and basket trays, I designed an assortment of copper trays in various sizes of hearts, rounds, rectangles, and squares. The maintenance of these trays is comparable to silver (they must be polished with copper polish before each use), but they look so beautiful and different that the effort is worthwhile. Oval Shaker-style trays made of cherry wood are also favorite serving pieces. They, too, come in a variety of sizes and can be decorated in many different ways. I often cover the entire tray with a single layer of galax leaves, or a layer of any other flat leaf, such as lemon leaves or ferns. Curly parsley, cut from its stems, makes a very sensible, cushiony bed for those hors d'oeuvres that have difficulty remaining upright during serving, such as filled cherry tomatoes or stuffed grapes. This "bed" is also a very good base for hors d'oeuvres that tend to be "greasy," such as dates wrapped with bacon or bacon-wrapped shrimp or scallops. The parsley remains fresh and crisp-looking when the food is removed.

It's important to give some time and attention to the presentation of drinks, too. The hors d'oeuvre party can be the occasion to use a collection of unusual glassware. For the past few years I have been collecting amethyst, green, and cobalt blue stemware, serving dishes, and flower containers, and I love to use them, singly or in combination, when entertaining guests. My brother George and his wife, Rita, also collect cobalt blue, and I sometimes borrow additional glasses from them if necessary. My sister Laura has a magnificent collection of pink Depression glassware, and her parties have a soft sparkle when she sets out her fantastic assortment of stemmed goblets. Wine connoisseurs may scoff at the use of colored glasses, but I find that unless I am serving a rare, cherished wine, I don't hesitate to be more unconventional in my use of glasses.

For large gatherings or receptions, or outdoor parties where breakage may occur, it's preferable to rent wonderful glasses that look as if they could be one's own. We deal with several excellent party rental agencies and never have difficulty finding appropriate glassware for parties. What we do that is somewhat different is to use traditional shapes and sizes of goblets in new and unusual ways. We serve sparkling kirs or margaritas in oversize bubble goblets and piña coladas

in Pilsner glasses; we rarely use standard on-the-rocks glasses or highball glasses. Mixed drinks are always served in stemmed bar glasses or wineglasses. For formal parties we will rent thin, imported, hand-blown crystal glasses, and for terrace parties or outdoor grilling parties, heavier, sturdier stemware.

The hors d'oeuvre party is truly an opportunity for a host or hostess to be imaginative. Creating finger food with care and attention to detail, developing ideas for unusual combinations and variations, using serving pieces, glassware, flowers, and other decorations in an original way—all of this makes hors d'oeuvres a fascinating art, and one, I find, that guests always enjoy and appreciate.

Smoked scallops and mussels, steamed giant shrimp, steamed red radishes, and a dipping sauce made of sour cream, balsamic vinegar, and grated radish are all slightly pink in color and look appetizing served on pink Depression glass plates, bowls, and an old dresser tray.

. . . .

CHAPTER ONE

Tea Party in the Library

Andy and I travel a great deal, and used to make two trips to Great Britain each year, for Andy's business primarily, but also for hiking through the Cotswolds, for driving through out-of-the-way towns and hamlets, and for extensive viewings of England's great gardens and stately homes. Each afternoon, about four or five o'clock, we made a habit of seeking out high tea. Often we forgot about lunch, preferring to wait for the extraordinary offerings of tearooms or small hotels. Even in London it became a habit to lunch late, at Brown's or the Savoy, on delicate tea sandwiches, scones, and crumpets.

More and more Americans are adapting the English high tea to their own use in home entertaining. A lovely, gracious way to entertain indoors or out, the tea party has many uses: it is wonderful as an occasion in itself, for a wedding reception, as a christening party, an engagement party, or a graduation. It is most beautiful if slightly formal in its appearance; that is, using silver, flowers, white or pastel linens, porcelain or glass teacups, crystal sherry glasses. The tea party permits us to use old silver tea sets that generally are relegated to the closet and wrappings of plastic and flannel.

Tea party food is based in strict tradition, but the variations of tradition are limitless. Scones, for example, can be studded with brandy-plumped currants or a sprinkling of caraway seeds, and can be cut into heart shapes or stars. Tiny biscuits can be flavored with dill, chives, or caraway seeds. Shortbread can be sweet or savory, flavored with vanilla bean, lemon peel, citron, or even cayenne pepper. Bowls of cream can be the authentic rich clotted cream from Devon, or whipped crème fraîche, or sour cream sweetened with brown sugar and a few drops of vanilla. Hard-boiled eggs are more fun if the eggs are from quails or Bantams or plovers than from full-grown hens. Some of the eggs can be left in the shell, to be peeled at leisure; others can be pickled in a light vinegar brine.

The paper-thin English tea sandwich, made from crustless white bread, has infinite possibilities for creativity. Don't eliminate the very delicious cucumber-mayonnaise, watercress and sweet butter, sliced breast of chicken-tomato combinations found at the Dorchester, but do invent new combinations. The only steadfast rule when composing these edibles—the bread *must* be very, very thinly sliced and must be *crustless!* Of course, it can be whole-wheat, grainy pumpernickel, or Russian black bread. And the toppings must be impeccably fresh and as thinly sliced as possible.

The actual tea service takes some thought. Tea is best when freshly brewed. Hot water should never be added to a teapot in which tea has already been brewed. Always pour out the dregs and make new tea. For a small gathering, a basic 8- or 10-cup tea service is sufficient. Provide one pot of tea; one pot of hot water to thin poured, brewed tea; pitchers of hot and cold milk, half-and-half, or cream; crystal and granular sugar; and, of course, thinly sliced lemons, which can be studded with cloves. For a larger group, a tea samovar is excellent. Many are fitted with small kerosene lights for warmth, and the spout is often easier to use than a teapot. Be sure there is one person in charge of the tea service, so that the tea is always hot and fresh.

Everything except the sandwiches can be prepared in advance. The sandwich making can be facilitated by having all the ingredients sliced and cut up beforehand and kept well wrapped and refrigerated if necessary. If the party is for a large group, twenty or more (as this one was), I suggest you have some help in assembling the sandwiches so that they can be served fresh during the party. You should allow approximately 2 of each type of hors d'oeuvre for your guests, and double that for the tea sandwiches.

Tea parties are usually called for four o'clock. Of course, depending on the occasion and location, the party may be earlier or later, the food more substantial or lighter, and the duration long or short. I prefer teas to last about two hours and always call them for 4:00 to 6:00 P.M. Menus can vary from all sweet to all savory or a mixture of the two. To make the party even more special, request that guests come attired in garden dress of the Victorian era, or black tie if the tea is to be held indoors, in winter. In that case, a tray of champagne cocktails could be served.

→》《←

Menu
for Twenty

TEA SANDWICHES · HERB SAVORIES
HEART-SHAPED SHORTBREAD FLAVORED WITH CAYENNE
SCONES WITH HERB JELLIES
CREAM PUFFS WITH JAM AND POWDERED SUGAR
BISCUITS WITH WHIPPED CRÈME FRAÎCHE
DEVILED EGGS · PICKLED QUAIL EGGS
HARD-BOILED QUAIL EGGS WITH SEASONED SALT
TEAS · COFFEE · SHERRY

Tea Sandwiches

Pain de Mie (page 158) or extra-thin bread (30 slices per pound), white, whole-wheat, pumpernickel, or black whole-grain

Unsalted butter, at room temperature

Homemade or Herb Mayonnaise (page 20 and page 96)

TOPPINGS

Watercress

Steamed, peeled shrimp cut in half lengthwise, mache or watercress leaves, fresh coriander

Japanese or red radish, watercress or cucumber, mustard sprouts or chives

Tomato, cucumber, flat Italian parsley

Cucumber and fresh dill

Sliced egg, cucumber, and chives

Sliced tomato and mashed avocado

Smoked salmon, olive slices, and watercress

Smoked turkey and cranberry jelly

Avocado slices and crumbled bacon

Cut off bread crusts. Using a serrated knife or cookie cutter, cut short

Dainty open-faced tea sandwiches are arranged on a pierced gallery-etched tray. The topping combinations are limitless, but always use only the freshest ingredients.

. . . .

stacks of bread into desired shapes (rectangles, rounds, triangles, etc.). Keep the bread covered with plastic wrap while you assemble the sandwiches so it does not dry out.

Lightly butter one side of bread, and spread with a plain or flavored homemade mayonnaise. Top with your choice of fillings to make assorted sandwiches.

Homemade Mayonnaise

MAKES 2½ CUPS

Prepare several kinds of homemade mayonnaise the day before your tea: plain, curry, red pepper, and herb mayonnaise are good flavors for tea sandwiches. A half-pint of each will be sufficient.

2 **eggs**
¼ **teaspoon dry mustard**
¾ **teaspoon salt**
2 **tablespoons freshly squeezed lemon juice**
1 **cup light olive oil**
1 **cup vegetable or safflower oil**

Put the eggs, mustard, salt, and lemon juice in the bowl of a food processor or a blender jar.

Combine the olive oil and vegetable oil. Turn on the machine and pour in the oil, drop by drop, until the mixture thickens. Add the remaining oil in a steady stream. Cover and refrigerate.

VARIATIONS: One teaspoon mild curry or 1 red pepper (roasted, seeded, and puréed) can be added to the mayonnaise.

→»≪←

Herb Mayonnaise

See page 96.

→»≪←

Herb Savories

MAKES 60 TO 70 SAVORIES

These are a very simple but pretty ''sandwich-type'' hors d'oeuvre. I was first served them at the home of Marina Schinz as an accompaniment to a morel soup.

1 **loaf Pain de Mie (page 158) or a good store-bought white bread, sliced very thin**
½ **pound (2 sticks) unsalted butter, at room temperature**
1 **cup finely minced delicate-flavored fresh herbs (chervil, dill, parsley, summer savory, coriander), watercress, or spring onions.**

Remove the crust from the bread and, using a biscuit or cookie cutter, cut the slices into various shapes.

Spread the butter on both sides and press the bread into the chopped herbs. Chill between two sheets of wax paper until ready to use.

→»≪←

Heart-shaped Shortbread Flavored with Cayenne

MAKES 10 4-INCH HEARTS

Shortbread can be baked in a variety of pans and molds. These cookies were baked in tin candy molds.

½ **pound (2 sticks) unsalted butter, at room temperature**
8 **tablespoons superfine sugar**
3 **cups all-purpose flour**

½ **teaspoon cayenne pepper Butter and sugar to line molds**

Preheat the oven to 350°.

With a wooden spoon or in an electric mixer, cream together the butter and sugar until very smooth.

Sift the flour into the butter mixture and, using your fingers, work all ingredients into a crumbly but very fine mixture. At this point, add the cayenne pepper, or your choice of other flavorings.

Butter the molds and dust the bottom and sides with sugar. Press the shortbread dough into the molds.

Bake until golden brown. The time varies from 10 minutes up, depending on the size of the mold. Do *not* overbake. Cool on racks before unmolding.

VARIATIONS: To make the more traditional sweet shortbread, you can substitute a few drops of vanilla extract, ¼ cup minced candied citron or lemon peel, or 2 tablespoons ground blanched almonds for the cayenne pepper.

. . . .

Below: *Herb savories are best made with delicate young herbs such as chervil, dill, parsley, and chives.* Right: *The tea table was pleasantly crowded with an array of colorful finger foods served from Grandmother Gilbert's silver, which makes the table very special.*

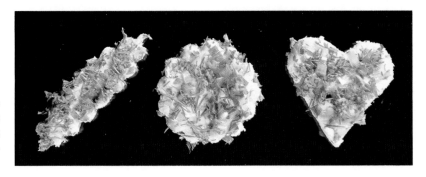

Pâte à choux puffs, scones, and biscuits are piled in silver filigree baskets. Silver-rimmed crystal ashtrays found a new use holding homemade herb-flavored jellies.

. . . .

Scones with Herb Jellies

MAKES ABOUT 40 1-INCH SCONES

4^1/$_2$	cups sifted all-purpose flour
2	teaspoons baking powder
^{1}/$_2$	teaspoon baking soda
2	tablespoons sugar
	Pinch of salt
^{1}/$_2$	pound (2 sticks) cold unsalted butter, cut into small pieces
1	to 1^1/$_4$ cups heavy cream

Butter for baking sheet

GLAZE

1	egg
^{1}/$_4$	cup light cream

Herb jellies: quince with thyme, currant with rosemary, or quince with sage, raspberries, and cinnamon

Preheat the oven to 375°.

Sift the dry ingredients into a large mixing bowl.

Cut the butter into the mixture with a pastry blender or two knives until the mixture resembles coarse meal. (This can also be done in a food processor, using half the flour mixture. Add to the remaining flour in bowl before adding cream.)

Mixing lightly with your fingers, add heavy cream just until the dough holds together. Wrap in plastic and chill about ^{1}/$_2$ hour before rolling out.

Roll the dough into a circle, ^{1}/$_2$ inch thick for small scones and ^{3}/$_4$ inch

thick for larger ones. Using a biscuit or cookie cutter, cut the dough into various shapes. (I used a heart-shaped cutter and a scalloped biscuit cutter for the scones pictured.)

Butter a large baking sheet and place the scones on it. Combine the egg and light cream in a bowl and brush the tops of the scones with the mixture.

Bake until golden brown and puffed, 13 to 15 minutes. Serve with herb jellies.

VARIATIONS: Savory scones can be made by adding ^{1}/$_4$ cup caraway seeds, ^{1}/$_4$ cup poppy seeds, or ^{1}/$_4$ cup finely chopped dill to the dough before adding cream.

Add ^{1}/$_4$ cup minced candied orange peel, or 1 cup currants soaked in 3 tablespoons brandy, to the dough for sweet scones.

Above: *Heart-shaped and fluted scones are lovely for tea—either with or without a filling of smoked turkey.* Above right: *Tiny chive biscuits—fluted and plain rounds— with country ham are another delicious tea savory.*

. . . .

Cream Puffs with Jam and Powdered Sugar

MAKES ABOUT 40 PUFFS

1   recipe Pâte à Choux Puffs
    (page 150)
1   pint homemade or
    good-quality raspberry,
    black raspberry, or grape
    jam
    Confectioners' sugar
    for dusting

Fill a pastry bag fitted with a number 7 round tip with your choice of jam.

Pierce one side of the puff with the tip and fill the puff, making sure it does not burst. If a pastry bag is not available, cut through the puff a third of the way from the top. Fill with jam and replace the top.

Put some powdered sugar in a fine sieve and dust the tops of the puffs.

Biscuits with Whipped Crème Fraîche

MAKES 75 TO 80 1¼-INCH
BISCUITS

6   cups sifted unbleached
    flour
¼   cup baking powder
1   teaspoon baking soda
¼   cup sugar
2   teaspoons salt
2   cups cold solid shortening
    or 1 cup each cold butter
    and shortening
1¼ to 1½ cups buttermilk
¼   cup heavy cream
    Crème Fraîche
    (page 60), whipped

Preheat the oven to 400°.

Combine all the dry ingredients and sift into a mixing bowl. Cut the shortening into the mixture with a pastry blender or two knives until it resembles rolled oats. Cover the mixture and chill for at least 20 minutes.

Add just enough buttermilk to the mixture to hold it together. Stir quickly with your hands until just combined. It does not matter if

some unincorporated flour is left in the bowl.

Put the dough on a lightly floured board and roll it into a rectangle, 1 inch thick, pressing crumbs into the dough. Fold the dough in half and roll it again into a rectangle ¾ inch to 1 inch thick. Cut into desired shapes and sizes with cookie or biscuit cutters and place on baking sheets lined with parchment. The biscuits will rise higher if they are placed close together on the baking sheets.

Brush the tops with cream and bake for 13 to 15 minutes, until slightly golden. Let cool on racks and serve with whipped crème fraîche.

VARIATIONS: Savory biscuits can be made by adding ¼ cup caraway seeds, ⅓ cup poppy seeds, ¼ cup chopped dill, or ⅓ cup chopped chives to the dough before adding buttermilk.

NOTE: Biscuits can be baked ahead of time and frozen. Put the biscuits in single layers between sheets of wax paper in airtight plastic containers. To use, thaw at room temperature and warm in a 350° oven.

Deviled eggs can be topped with caviar, chopped herbs, or coarse salt. The yolk mixture is prettiest when piped in with a decorative tip.

. . . .

Deviled Eggs

MAKES 20 HORS D'OEUVRES

- 10   hard-boiled eggs
- 1/2   cup Homemade
         Mayonnaise (page 20)
- 4   tablespoons (1/2 stick)
         unsalted butter, melted
         Salt and freshly ground
         black pepper to taste
         Pinch of cayenne pepper

Peel the eggs and cut in half, either lengthwise or crosswise. Carefully scoop out the yolks, and arrange the whites on a platter or tray. (You can set the eggs on a thick bed of dill, parsley, or other green to keep them from rolling.)

In the bowl of an electric mixer or food processor, blend the egg yolks, mayonnaise, and melted butter until smooth. Season to taste.

Put the egg yolk mixture in a pastry bag fitted with a large star tip. Pipe the mixture carefully and very neatly into the egg halves. Cover with plastic wrap and refrigerate until ready to use, up to 3 hours.

VARIATIONS: Two tablespoons Di-

jon mustard and/or 1 tablespoon curry powder, 1 to 2 tablespoons chopped fresh dill or chervil, or 1 to 2 tablespoons very finely chopped ham can be added to the blended yolk mixture.

Deviled eggs can be topped with a spoonful of red, black, or golden caviar.

⇢⇥⇤⇠

Hard-Boiled Quail Eggs with Seasoned Salt

Inez Norwich, a friend of mine who lives in Fairfield, Connecticut, raises quails. Her quail eggs are the ones pictured, and her recipe for pickled quail eggs is included below.

To hard-boil eggs, put room-temperature eggs in a heavy saucepan and cover with cold water. Bring to a gentle boil and cook for 4 to 5 minutes. Pour off the hot water and cool the eggs in cold water. Peel the eggs when they have cooled completely.

Serve with seasoned salt.

MAKES ABOUT 1/2 CUP

- 1/2   cup coarse salt
- 1   teaspoon coarsely ground
         white pepper
         Pinch of cayenne pepper
         Pinch of sweet paprika

Combine all ingredients and keep covered in a dry place.

⇢⇥⇤⇠

Pickled Quail Eggs

MAKES 4 CUPS BRINE, ENOUGH TO PICKLE 60 QUAIL EGGS

BRINE

- 1   cup white wine vinegar or
         champagne vinegar
- 3   cups water
- 1   tablespoon pickling spice
- 1   medium onion, minced

- 60   hard-boiled quail eggs

At least 5 days before serving, combine the vinegar, water, spice, and onion in a small saucepan. Bring to a boil and cook for 2 minutes. Strain the brine and reserve.

Peel the eggs and pack them into sterilized pint jars. Pour the hot brine over them, cover, and refrigerate for up to 2 months. You can also process the filled jars in a hot water bath for 10 minutes, or in a pressure cooker for 5 minutes to form an airtight vacuum seal. This way, eggs will be slightly tougher but will last a good deal longer.

NOTE: The brine recipe can be divided or multiplied as necessary.

. . . .

Right: *Tiny quail eggs—hard-boiled or pickled in a light brine—are very tender and interestingly different. Sherry was also offered in tall stemmed glasses.*

CHAPTER TWO

Christmas Cocktails

The underlying theme for this festive, small, and rather elegant Christmas party was the color scheme—red and green. The decorations, the garnishes for the trays, and the foods themselves were chosen with this theme in mind, with just a few minor deviations (white tortellini).

We used almost all silver trays for serving, making sure they were polished and gleaming the day before the party. One tuxedo-clad waiter, wearing white gloves, served the hors d'oeuvres, and another waiter served drinks from a bar set up in the pantry.

On a small sideboard in the dining room, candles in pewter holders and feathery red and green branches accented platters of baked oysters. Oyster plates were stacked next to the platters, and small forks were provided. All of the other hors d'oeuvres were served as finger food on trays decorated with

. . . .

The bar for an elaborate Victorian Christmas party is set up on tables swathed in ecru lace in the Metropolitan Museum of Art's American Wing.

the Christmas season in mind: small boughs of spruce, a Christmas tree composed of French seaweed, a wreath made from basil leaves and rosemary sprigs. Many other garnishes could be substituted—for example, sprigs of boxwood, ropes of juniper, strings of cranberries, kumquats, galax leaves, ivy, brightly colored flowers, red and green ribbons, traditional Christmas decorations such as tinsel and glass balls, bells and mistletoe. Old children's toys are sometimes fun to use as tray decorations, as are antique Christmas cards, and animals made of moss-covered wire. At a Christmas party at the Metropolitan Museum of Art we used whimsical moss rabbits and teddy bears and cranberries and nuts as the decorations on the trays.

This particular party was for eighteen guests. We made three of every hors d'oeuvre per person, with the exception of the oysters. Because they were served on oyster plates, we made six per guest. Cocktails lasted for an hour and a half, and the oysters were really a first course. The guests left the cocktail party and went to a sit-down dinner elsewhere, where dinner began with a hot soup course. If this had been a longer party, the menu could have been filled out to include heartier fare and more variety. It would be fun to keep in the holiday spirit and set out a Smithfield ham and tiny hot biscuits, a smoked turkey and some ginger muffins, cranberry relish, and trays of Christmas desserts—sugar cookies, mince tarts, plum puddings, some fruit-cakes, and possibly a croquembouche.

The wreath of olives can be arranged early in the day and refrigerated, the asparagus blanched and wrapped with prosciutto one to two hours before guests arrive. The cherry tomatoes and mousse and the pattypan squash and its filling can be readied hours before. The oysters and the tortellini require cooking during the party, but that can be done if all the other trays are decorated and ready beforehand. The crudités can be prepared early the day of the party.

Menu
for Eighteen

PATTYPAN SQUASH FILLED WITH RED PEPPER CHEESE
SKEWERED TORTELLINI WITH ROASTED GARLIC GARNISH
BAKED OYSTERS RED AND GREEN · SAVORY WREATH
CHERRY TOMATOES FILLED WITH SMOKED SALMON MOUSSE
ASPARAGUS WRAPPED WITH PROSCIUTTO
CARDINALES

We carried the red and green Christmas theme out as fully as possible. Here, tiny pattypan squash are filled with red pepper cheese and arranged on a "tree" of bright green seaweed. Below: *White and green tortellini are placed on 6-inch bamboo skewers.*

. . . .

Pattypan Squash Filled with Red Pepper Cheese

MAKES 40 HORS D'OEUVRES

RED PEPPER CHEESE FILLING

MAKES ABOUT 1½ CUPS

 1 **cup minced sweet red pepper**
½ **cup grated sharp Cheddar cheese**
 1 **egg, beaten**
 Salt and freshly ground black pepper to taste
 Pinch of cayenne pepper

40 **pattypan squashes, 1 inch to 1½ inches in diameter**

Preheat the oven to 375°.

Combine all the ingredients for the red pepper cheese filling and set aside until ready to use.

With the point of a small, sharp knife or a melon-ball scoop, hollow out the top part of each squash. Steam the squashes over boiling water for a minute or two, until barely tender. Do not overcook.

Spoon the filling into the hollowed-out squashes and put them on a cookie sheet. Bake until the cheese is melted and the filling is hot, about 5 minutes.

NOTE: Choose squashes no larger than 1½ inches in diameter. If you cannot find them, use ⅓-inch thick slices of zucchini or summer squash and hollow out the centers with a melon-ball scoop.

Skewered Tortellini with Roasted Garlic Garnish

See page 141.

➤➤❮❮

Roasted Garlic

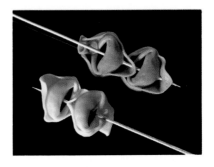

Roasted garlic tends to be sweeter and milder than raw or sautéed garlic and is even delicious as a vegetable. Make a lot of it and preserve it in olive oil for later use in salads and dips.

Preheat the oven to 350°.

Roast several heads of garlic, lightly sprinkled with olive oil, for about 1 hour, or until golden brown and soft.

Separate the cloves and store in a container filled with olive oil.

Above left: *The skewered tortellini were piled onto a glistening silver tray, served with a small bowl of Parmesan dipping sauce, and garnished with whole heads of roast garlic.* Above right: *Baked oysters are set atop wilted spinach leaves and decorated with a red strip of sun-dried tomato.*

· ·

Baked Oysters Red and Green

  2   **to 3 oysters per person**
  ¹⁄₂ **cup olive oil**
  ¹⁄₄ **teaspoon dried red pepper flakes**

PER OYSTER

  1 **large spinach leaf**
  1 **or 2 strips of sun-dried tomatoes or pimientos**

Combine the olive oil and red pepper flakes. Set aside.

Steam the spinach until just wilted, about 2 minutes. Drain well.

Preheat the oven to 350°.

Loosen the oysters from their shells and slip a spinach leaf underneath. Top each with a strip or two of sun-dried tomato.

Bake the oysters for 3 to 4 minutes, sprinkle with the olive oil-red pepper mixture, and serve immediately.

→≫≪←

Savory Wreath

This platter is an interesting and unexpected arrangement of olives, cornichons, pumate, and herbs.

On the fresh basil leaves arranged around the perimeter of a round silver tray we placed an assortment of olives—Sicilian, French, Moroccan, and Greek. Sprigs of fresh rosemary add to the design, which is accented by pumate, sour French pickles (cornichons), and roasted peppers.

You could also add quartered baby artichokes, artichoke hearts, marinated mushrooms, and any other pickled or marinated vegetables. Any available

herbs could be used as well—oregano, dill, parsley, or sage.

→≫≪←

Cherry Tomatoes Filled with Smoked Salmon Mousse

MAKES 60 HORS D'OEUVRES

  60 **red, firm cherry tomatoes (about 2 pints) Smoked Salmon Mousse (page 72)**

GARNISH
Fresh dill

Wash and dry the cherry tomatoes. With a sharp serrated knife, cut off the round bottom of each tomato. Remove the seeds and pulp with a small melon-ball scoop and put the tomatoes, cut side down, on a rack

Above left: *The savory wreath is arranged on sprigs of fresh herbs and basil leaves.* Above right: *Ripe, red cherry tomatoes filled with a mixture of smoked salmon and cream cheese rest on a bed of green dill.*

. . . .

or on paper towels to drain. Refrigerate until ready to use. (Cutting off the bottom of the tomatoes and standing them on the stem end makes them less apt to roll.)

To serve, soften the mousse with a wooden spoon and put it in a pastry bag fitted with a star tip. Pipe the mixture into the cherry tomatoes and garnish with a sprig of fresh dill. Serve on a bed of lettuce leaves, kale greens, parsley, or dill to keep the tomatoes from rolling.

Filling Variations

STEAK TARTARE

MAKES 40 HORS D'OEUVRES

- ½ **pound freshly ground sirloin**
- 2 **tablespoons small capers**
- 1 **garlic clove, pressed**
- 1 **egg yolk**

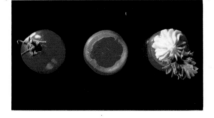

A cherry tomato is easily hollowed out with a melon-ball scoop or small spoon and the salmon mousse piped in with a decorative tip pastry bag.

. . . .

- 2 **scallions, minced**
  Salt and freshly ground black pepper to taste

GARNISH
  Curly parsley

Combine all ingredients except parsley in a mixing bowl. Fill toma-

toes with a bit of the meat mixture. Garnish with a leaf of curly parsley.

VARIATIONS: Other types of tartares can be made by substituting the following for the sirloin: ½ pound fresh salmon fillet cut into ¼-inch cubes; ½ pound freshly ground veal, 1 additional tablespoon small capers, and 2 tablespoons minced fennel leaves; or ½ pound fresh fillet of sole and 1 tablespoon chopped coriander.

ANCHOVY FILLING

MAKES 40 HORS D'OEUVRES

- 40 **anchovy fillets**
- 40 **small capers**
- ¼ **cup grated Parmesan cheese**

Roll each anchovy around a caper and stuff into a hollowed-out cherry tomato. Sprinkle with Parmesan cheese.

ARTICHOKES AND HEARTS OF PALM

MAKES 60 HORS D'OEUVRES

   1   *16-ounce can of artichoke hearts, drained*
   1   *16-ounce can of hearts of palm, drained*
        Juice of 1 lemon
 ¼   *cup tarragon vinegar*
 ⅓   *cup olive oil*
 ¼   *cup chopped fresh dill*
 ¼   *cup chopped Italian flat-leaf parsley*
        Freshly ground black pepper to taste

Put the artichoke hearts and hearts of palm in the bowl of a food processor and chop coarsely.

In a medium mixing bowl, combine the lemon juice, vinegar, and olive oil and stir in the chopped artichoke hearts and hearts of palm. Add dill and parsley, stir to combine, and season to taste.

Spoon the mixture into cherry tomatoes and serve.

CORN SALAD

MAKES 40 HORS D'OEUVRES

   1   *cup cooked corn kernels*
   2   *tablespoons chopped fresh basil*
   2   *scallions, minced*
   2   *tablespoons finely chopped red bell pepper*
 ¼   *cup olive oil*
   1   *tablespoon hot chili oil*
        Salt and freshly ground black pepper to taste

Combine all ingredients in a mixing bowl. Fill tomatoes with a bit of the mixture.

MOZZARELLA AND OLIVE OIL

MAKES 40 HORS D'OEUVRES

 ½   *pound fresh mozzarella cheese, cut into ¼-inch cubes*

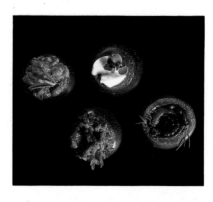

Cherry tomatoes can be stuffed with a variety of fillings. Clockwise from top right: *Mozarella and olive oil garnished with tiny basil leaves; anchovy and caper with dill; steak tartare with curly parsley; and salmon tartare with a fresh rosemary garnish.*

. . . .

   2   *tablespoons chopped pumate (sun-dried tomatoes)*
 ¼   *cup olive oil*
        Freshly ground black pepper to taste
   1   *tablespoon chopped fresh basil leaves*

Marinate the cheese and pumate in olive oil and pepper for several hours before stuffing into tomatoes. Sprinkle with basil.

PESTO PASTA

MAKES 40 HORS D'OEUVRES

   1   *cup cooked small pasta (tiny bow ties or angel hair)*
 ¼   *cup olive oil*
 ¼   *cup minced fresh basil*
   1   *garlic clove, minced*
   2   *tablespoons grated Parmesan cheese*
        Salt and freshly ground black pepper to taste

Combine all ingredients in a mixing bowl. Fill tomatoes with a bit of the mixture.

Asparagus Wrapped with Prosciutto

Allow 2 to 3 asparagus stalks per guest. Trim the asparagus (use medium-size asparagus, which are easier to wrap than the very thin ones) and blanch them until just tender (2 to 4 minutes) in a large kettle of boiling water). Immerse the blanched asparagus in ice water to cool them, drain them well, and keep them refrigerated until you are ready to wrap. To serve, cut very thinly sliced prosciutto into thirds lengthwise and wrap these strips around the stems of the asparagus.

→>><<<

Cardinale

MAKES 1 DRINK

This is basically a red wine kir, named, I suppose, for the brilliant red color of a cardinal's robes. It looks very pretty garnished with a slice of orange, too, instead of the lemon peel.

   8   *ounces red wine*
   1   *tablespoon imported crème de cassis (black currant liqueur)*
        Thin strip of lemon peel

Place a couple of ice cubes in a large bubble goblet. Pour the wine and cassis over the ice and add the lemon peel.

VARIATION: Fill the goblet to the top with Perrier or sparkling water.

. . . .

Right: *On a glistening silver tray, golden freesias and yellow peppers are a colorful counterpoint to a pyramid of bright green blanched asparagus that are wrapped with paper-thin slices of prosciutto.*

CHAPTER THREE

Country Kitchen Hors d'Oeuvres

My sister, Kathy Evans, lives with her husband, Mark, and two little boys in Old Greenwich, Connecticut, in a very charming, comfortable home. She is very busy, having combined the raising of a family with her work as a weaver and designer. Her work is displayed everywhere in her home: hooked rugs adorn tabletops and doorsteps; rag runners cover walls, floors, and tables; and pastel shawls and throws add cozy touches to sofas and chairs.

When Kathy entertains, which is frequently, she often chooses to set a buffet in the country kitchen. There, an array of inspired finger foods can be displayed amid bright flowers and gaily colored woven rugs in the warm sunlight of late afternoon.

This particular cocktail party for twenty-four guests was held from five to eight one early spring afternoon. It was a weekend, so Kathy had the benefit of lots of ''help'' from her four- and six-year-old sons (which is why almost everything had to be prepared the week before!). The menu is clever in that it leaves very little for the last minute. Only the frittatas have to be baked just before serving, but since the vegetables had been precooked and arranged in the baking dishes, what remained was only beating a few eggs and baking. Meanwhile, the guests savored the other good things—pâtés, rillettes, an assortment of unusual cheeses, mounds of asparagus vinaigrette, and baskets of warm, crispy breads.

Tiny red potatoes are baked in the hot oven along with the frittatas and served with a variety of toppings. They are a simple, comforting food and extremely popular.

. . . .

A sun-filled kitchen is a delightful setting for this party. The buffet table is laden with cheeses, fruits, flowers, and a bright yellow platter heaped with asparagus vinaigrette.

Since we first started serving little potatoes, we have been able to make the eating of them easier. Rather than putting out whole hot potatoes, some of which might be a bit too large for one or two bites, we cut the potatoes in half, arrange them cut side down on trays, and scoop out the tops with a melon-ball scoop. The hollow is filled with any of the toppings, in this case sautéed onions, roasted walnuts, sour cream, and alfalfa sprouts.

One large table was used for the cheeses, which were perfectly ripe and chosen for their unusual shapes and flavors, breads, ripe fruits, imported French butter, and spring asparagus. Kathy had spread a cotton rag runner on the table and arranged masses of California poppies in a pinkware bowl. The trays and platters were an eclectic mix of basketry, bread boards, spatterware, and twig mats. A black iron chestnut pan displayed a great number of freshly roasted chestnuts, which were eagerly peeled and consumed by the guests. (The chestnuts were roasted in the fireplace in the adjoining room.)

Another table was used for the serving of the baby potatoes and fillings. Yet another table was the pâté buffet, where decorative pâté dishes and pottery terrines held rillettes and country pâtés. This menu includes three of Sara Foster's fabulous pâtés: duck, chicken and veal, and a country pâté. Sara doesn't believe you must stick with a specific recipe: she suggests that you alter the design and decoration of the pâté according to your own whims. Ingredients, too, may be varied according to what you have available, or according to your own taste. Herbs and spices, especially, can be changed or added. It is of utmost importance to *taste* each pâté before the whole is cooked. Make a patty of the raw mixture and lightly sauté it in unflavored oil. The patty should taste intensely of the flavorings. The flavors will mellow as the pâté ripens, a process that takes two to four days. What seems to be spicy will be just right after the pâté cooks.

Kathy loves wine, and only white French Burgundies were served at this party. It was a friendly, hearty cocktail buffet, and the high quality of the homemade foods and the carefully chosen cheeses and wines made it a party to remember.

→»«←

Menu

for Twenty-four

CROQUE MONSIEUR · DUCK RILLETTES

APPLES WITH CHICKEN LIVER PÂTÉ · DUCK PÂTÉ

CHICKEN AND VEAL PÂTÉ · COUNTRY PÂTÉ

HOMEMADE FRENCH BREAD · GALANTINE OF DUCK

FRITTATAS · ASPARAGUS VINAIGRETTE

TINY PIZZAS · BAKED RED POTATOES WITH TOPPINGS

APRICOTS WITH BLEU DE BRESSE

FRUIT BREADS · ASSORTED CHEESES

FRENCH WHITE BURGUNDY WINES

Croque Monsieur

MAKES 60 HORS D'OEUVRES

These are little ham-and-cheese sandwiches that can be made from a variety of breads and fillings.

1	1-pound loaf of white or whole-wheat bread, cut into 30 thin slices
½	pound (2 sticks) unsalted butter, melted
⅓	cup Dijon mustard
1½	pounds good boiled ham, thinly sliced
1½	pounds Swiss cheese, thinly sliced

Brush one side of each slice of bread with butter and spread mustard on the other side. Layer one slice of ham and one of cheese on the mustard-coated side, making sure to cover the entire surface. Cover with a slice of bread, buttered side up. (At this point you can wrap the croque monsieur and refrigerate overnight, or until ready to use.)

Heat a griddle or a large, heavy frying pan and grill the sandwiches over low heat for about 4 minutes on each side, or until golden brown. While cooking, press the sandwich with a weight such as another frying pan or with a spatula.

Remove the sandwiches from the heat. Cut off the crusts and cut each trimmed sandwich into triangles or rectangles. Serve immediately.

VARIATIONS: Prosciutto, smoked turkey, Black forest ham, or dried beef can be substituted for boiled ham.

Brie, St. André, Camembert, Cheddar, or herb Brie can be substituted for Swiss cheese.

Finely chopped chutney and other relishes make excellent condiments.

Sprinkle the ungrilled ham and cheese with finely chopped chervil or parsley.

A duck decoy watches over an earthenware terrine filled with rillettes of duck and an accompanying basket piled with slices of homemade French bread.

. . . .

Duck Rillettes

MAKES 2½ POUNDS

1	6-pound duck
⅓	bottle of dry white wine
1	onion, sliced
1	bay leaf
1	garlic clove, peeled
	Thyme sprigs
	Salt and freshly ground black pepper
	Clarified butter

Quarter the duck. Brown in a heavy roasting pan in a 400° oven until the fat begins to melt, about 30 minutes. Turn the pieces to brown evenly.

Remove duck from the oven, add the remaining ingredients except the butter, and cover. Cook slowly on top of the stove for 3½ hours.

Strain the juices and fat from the pan. Shred the meat into small pieces and finely chop the skin. Discard the bones. Add the meat and skin to the strained fatty liquid and beat well with a wooden spoon. Taste for seasonings (pepper improves the flavor immensely). Chill in the refrigerator, stirring with the wooden spoon every 30 minutes, until the rillettes are very stiff. Pack into earthenware crocks and seal with clarified butter. This helps preserve the rillettes. Cover tightly. Keep refrigerated until 1 hour before serving.

To serve, scrape off the butter, put the crock on a tray, ad surround with thin slices of French bread.

Apples with Chicken Liver Pâté

MAKES 100 HORS D'OEUVRES

CHICKEN LIVER PÂTÉ WITH CURRANTS

MAKES 2 CUPS

- 1/3 **cup currants**
- 2 **tablespoons cognac**
- 3 **tablespoons port**
- 6 **tablespoons (3/4 stick) unsalted butter, at room temperature**
- 1 **pound chicken livers, cleaned**
- 1 **garlic clove, minced**
- 1 **teaspoon salt, or to taste Pepper to taste**
- 1/2 **teaspoon fresh thyme Melted duck fat or clarified butter**
- 12 **Golden or Red Delicious apples**

To make the pâté, soak the currants in the cognac and port overnight.

Melt 3 tablespoons of butter in a skillet over medium-high heat and sauté the livers for about 5 minutes. Do not overcook them; the centers should remain pink. Remove the chicken livers with a slotted spoon and put them into a food processor.

Drain the currants and add the cognac mixture to the skillet. Add the garlic, salt, pepper, and thyme and cook for 1 minute over medium-high heat. Pour over the chicken livers and process until well combined and smooth.

Stir in the remaining butter and the currants, adjust seasoning with salt and pepper, and pack the pâté into a 2-cup terrine. Seal with 1/4 inch of melted duck fat or clarified butter. Refrigerate for at least 2 days.

Core the apples with a long apple corer, being careful to take out the entire core with one single cut. Cut each apple in half lengthwise, and

place the cut side down and cut each half crosswise into 1/4-inch-thick slices.

To serve, scrape the fat or butter off the pâté. Spread the pâté on the apple slices with a metal spatula. Pâté can be garnished with alfalfa or mustard sprouts, watercress leaves, mache leaves, or a tiny sprig of parsley, if desired.

VARIATIONS: 1/2 pound chicken livers and 1/2 pound duck livers can be substituted for the pound of chicken livers.

Pâté can also be spread on pear slices, bread, or toast.

Variation

CHICKEN LIVER PÂTÉ

MAKES 2 CUPS

- 1 **pound chicken livers**
- 3 **tablespoons chopped onion**
- 1 **medium Granny Smith apple, peeled and chopped**
- 1/2 **pound (2 sticks) unsalted butter plus 1 tablespoon, at room temperature**
- 1 **teaspoon dry mustard**

- 1/4 **teaspoon salt**
- 1/4 **teaspoon grated nutmeg Dash each of cayenne pepper and ground cloves**
- 3 **tablespoons clarified butter**

GARNISH
Sprouts

Trim the chicken livers of all fat. Put in a small saucepan and cover with water. Bring to a boil, then reduce heat and simmer for 20 minutes. Cool in the liquid and drain.

Sauté the onion and apple in 1 tablespoon butter over medium heat for 5 minutes.

In a food processor or blender, combine the livers, remaining 1/2 pound butter, onion, apple, and seasonings. Blend until very smooth. Pack into a terrine or

. . . .

Green Anjou pears, sliced lengthwise, are topped with piped chicken liver pâté and garnished with enoki mushrooms and sprouts.

earthenware bowl and top with melted clarified butter.

To serve, scrape off the clarified butter and pipe or spread the pâté onto apple slices. (Piping is easier if the pâté is mixed well with an electric mixer or wooden spoon before being put into a pastry bag.) Decorate with sprouts if desired.

→≫≪←

Duck Pâté

MAKES 2 6-CUP TERRINES

1½	pounds duck meat, cut in strips
1¼	cups brandy
¾	pound ground veal
¾	pound ground pork
1¼	pounds ground bacon
1	onion, minced
1	shallot, minced
1	pear, peeled, cored, and finely chopped
3	eggs, lightly beaten
¼	cup chopped fresh parsley
1	tablespoon salt
3	garlic cloves, minced
1	teaspoon ginger
2	teaspoons allspice
1	tablespoon freshly ground black pepper
1	pound caul fat
½	pound duck meat, cut into strips
½	pound duck liver, cut into strips
1	cup dried apricots, soaked in brandy
1	cup shelled pistachio nuts

Marinate the strips of duck meat in 1 cup of brandy for 2 to 3 days.

Preheat the oven to 325°.

Grind the marinated duck meat (reserving 10 small strips for decoration) and combine with the rest of the meats in a mixing bowl. Add the onion, shallot, and pear.

In another mixing bowl combine the eggs, remaining ¼ cup brandy, parsley, salt, garlic, ginger, allspice, and pepper. Stir in the meat mixture and blend well.

Line two 6-cup pâté molds with strips of caul fat and pack half the pâté mixture into the molds. Place strips of duck meat, liver, apricots, and pistachios down the center of the mixture in a decorative pattern. Cover with the remaining pâté mixture and top with caul fat.

Cover the pâté with foil and place it in a baking pan. Fill the pan with boiling water and bake the pâté for 2 hours, or until the internal temperature reaches 135° to 140°. Remove from the oven and let cool.

Place some weights on top of the pâté and refrigerate overnight, or up to 2 days. Unmold and serve at room temperature.

NOTE: Caul fat is available in pork markets. Thinly sliced fat back can also be used as a lining for the pâté molds.

It's especially useful to keep a container of brandy-soaked dried fruits available in the refrigerator for making pâtés, breads, biscuits, scones, etc.

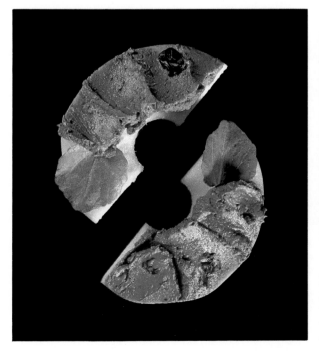

Left: *An apple slice is the base for chicken liver pâté made with cognac-soaked currants. Spread on with a spatula, the pâté is garnished with a leaf of watercress.* Right: *An unusual but eminently delicious combination of duck pâté on carrot bread.*

Chicken and Veal Pâté

MAKES 1 LARGE 8-CUP TERRINE

> ¾ pound ground fresh veal
> ¾ pound ground chicken
> ½ pound ground pork fat
> ½ pound ground bacon
> ½ cup bread crumbs
> 2 teaspoons freshly ground black pepper
> 1 tablespoon salt
> 1 teaspoon allspice
> 4 garlic cloves, peeled and minced
> ½ cup cognac
> 4 eggs, lightly beaten
> 1 onion, minced
> 2 bunches of fresh spinach
> ¼ cup clarified butter
> ½ pound chicken livers
> ½ cup walnut halves
> 1 bunch of chives

Preheat the oven to 300°.

Combine the veal, chicken, pork fat, bacon, and bread crumbs in a mixing bowl.

In another mixing bowl, combine the pepper, salt, allspice, garlic, cognac, eggs, and onion. Stir in the meat mixture and blend well. Set aside.

Bring a large pot of water to a boil, and drop in the spinach for 10 seconds, just long enough to wilt the leaves. Drain and dry on paper towels.

. . . .

Pottery terrines and yellowware pie dishes hold the sliced pâtés and galantine of duck, which are garnished with full sprigs of fresh herbs. Cornichons and herb-and-spice-flavored mustards served from spatterware custard cups and stoneware pots accompany the pâtés (clockwise from top right): chicken and veal pâté, country pâté, galantine of duck, and duck pâté.

Brush an 8-cup pâté mold with clarified butter and line it with half the wilted spinach leaves. Pack half of the meat mixture into the mold. Place the chicken livers down the center and arrange the walnuts and chives on both sides to create a design. Cover with the remaining mixture and top with more spinach leaves. Brush with clarified butter.

Cover the pâté with foil and put it in a baking pan. Fill the pan with boiling water and bake the pâté for 2 hours, or until the internal temperature reaches 135° to 140°. Remove from the oven.

Place some weights on top of the pâté and refrigerate overnight, or up to 2 days.

Unmold the pâté and serve at room temperature.

NOTE: Freezing is not generally recommended for pâtés. Meat pâtés do improve in flavor if refrigerated for 2 or 3 days; they will keep for up to 7 days.

VARIATION: Use thinly sliced bacon to line the terrine in place of spinach.

—»›‹«—

Country Pâté

MAKES 2 6-CUP TERRINES

> 1 pound ground veal
> 2 pounds ground pork
> 1½ pounds ground rabbit
> 2 pounds ground pork fat
> 1 medium onion, minced
> 2 shallots, minced
> 6 garlic cloves, minced
> 2 apples, peeled, cored, and ground
> 1 tablespoon dried thyme
> 1 tablespoon allspice
> 1 tablespoon salt
> 1 tablespoon freshly ground black pepper

> 1 cup brandy
> 4 eggs, lightly beaten
> 12 crushed juniper berries
> 1 pound sliced bacon or caul fat
> 10 pitted prunes, soaked in brandy
> ½ pound lean rabbit meat, cut into strips
> ½ cup whole hazelnuts

Preheat the oven to 325°.

In a large mixing bowl, combine all the ground meats, onion, shallots, garlic, and apples.

In another mixing bowl combine the thyme, allspice, salt, pepper, brandy, eggs, and juniper berries. Add to the meat mixture and stir well.

Line one large 10-cup loaf pan or two small (6 cups each) pâté molds with caul fat. Pack half of the mixture into the mold and arrange the prunes down the center, with the strips of rabbit and hazelnuts on both sides. Cover with the remaining mixture and top with caul fat.

Cover the pâté with foil and put it in a baking pan. Fill the pan with boiling water and bake the pâté for 2 hours, or until the internal temperature reaches 135° to 140°. Remove from the oven and let cool.

Place some weights on top of the pâté and refrigerate overnight, or up to 2 days. Unmold and serve at room temperature.

NOTE: Weighting the cooked pâté is very important, since it eliminates excess liquid and compresses the pâté, which permits better slicing and a nicer presentation.

—»›‹«—

Homemade French Bread

See page 159.

Galantine of Duck

MAKES ABOUT 30 SLICES

1/4	pound ground duck meat
1	egg
1	tablespoon ground fresh sage leaves
1	teaspoon salt
2	teaspoons freshly ground black pepper
1/4	teaspoon grated nutmeg
3	tablespoons brandy
1	large duck breast, boned (about 1 1/2 to 2 pounds)
1/4	pound thinly sliced prosciutto
7	dried apples or figs, soaked in brandy
1/8	cup shelled pistachio nuts Cheesecloth and cotton string
3	tablespoons olive oil
1	quart duck or chicken stock
1	cup white wine

Combine the duck meat, egg, sage, salt, pepper, nutmeg, and brandy in a mixing bowl. Set aside.

Place the duck breast skin side down on a work surface and flatten it with a meat pounder. Butterfly each side of the breast and pound the meat to make it an even thickness to cover the entire skin surface. Try to shape it into a rectangle.

Arrange several layers of prosciutto, covering the entire surface of the breast. Place half of the ground mixture, lengthwise, all the way down the center of the breast to form a line about 1 inch wide. Arrange the fruit and pistachios in a pattern in the center of the ground mixture. Cover with the remaining ground meat.

Roll the breast into a cylinder, completely encasing the ground mixture. Wrap the galantine tightly in cheesecloth and tie the ends to secure. To protect the shape, tie the galantine every 2 to 3 inches along the length with string.

In a pot large enough to hold the galantine, heat the olive oil over medium-high heat and brown the breast on all sides. Add the stock and wine, bring to a boil, lower to a simmer, and poach the galantine for 30 to 40 minutes, depending on the size, turning often. Remove from the broth and let cool. Refrigerate overnight before serving.

To serve, remove cheesecloth and cut 1/4-inch-thick slices and arrange them in overlapping rows on a tray.

⇉⇇

Frittatas

MAKES 3 8-INCH OMELETTES

1/2	cup olive oil
2	medium onions, peeled and thinly sliced
2	potatoes, peeled and thinly sliced
8	mushrooms, sliced
10	asparagus tips, steamed
1	red pepper, seeded and sliced
1	zucchini, thinly sliced
12	eggs, beaten Salt and freshly ground black pepper Fresh sage leaves, to taste

Preheat the oven to 400°.

Divide the olive oil among three baking dishes. Arrange some onion slices at the bottom of each baking dish and bake for 6 minutes. Cover with potatoes and bake for 8 minutes. Arrange the remaining vegetables in a decorative pattern and bake for another 5 minutes. Pour the eggs over the vegetables and season with salt and pepper and sage. The eggs should come to within 1/4 inch of the top of the dish.

Bake for 15 to 20 minutes, until the center of the frittata is set and the sides are puffy and golden. Reduce the oven temperature if the eggs

brown too quickly. Do not overcook, or the eggs will get tough.

Let cool slightly before slicing into small wedges.

NOTE: Other herbs such as thyme, chervil, dill, or summer savory may be used as a substitute for the sage.

⇉⇇

Asparagus Vinaigrette

MAKES 24 TO 30 SERVINGS

3	pounds pencil-thin or very small asparagus

VINAIGRETTE

MAKES 1 1/2 CUPS

2	egg yolks
1	cup vegetable oil
3	tablespoons sour cream
3	tablespoons chopped fresh tarragon
1	tablespoon Dijon mustard
1	tablespoon tarragon or white wine vinegar

Bring a large pot of lightly salted water to a boil. Add the asparagus and cook for 3 to 5 minutes. Drain them and plunge into ice water to cool. Drain and refrigerate, covered, until ready to use.

To make the vinaigrette, put the egg yolks in a mixing bowl. Slowly whisk the oil into the egg yolk until thick and creamy. Add the remaining ingredients and chill until ready to use.

To serve, mound the asparagus on a platter and pour on the vinaigrette.

· · · · · · · · · · · ·

Three puffy vegetable frittatas, hot from the oven, await slicing on a table covered with green and white homespun cloth. A large green Fiestaware bowl is filled with fragrant, yellow dill flowers.

Opposite: *Some of Kathy's collection of colored glass brightens a serving table that displays halved new potatoes topped with a dab of sour cream and walnuts and additional toppings of sprouts and sautéed onions. A yellowware basket holds an arrangement of pink artemesia.*

· · · · · · · · · · · ·

Baked Red Potatoes with Toppings

See page 142.

→≫≪←

Tiny Pizzas

MAKES 30 3-INCH PIZZAS

PIZZA DOUGH

1	package of dry yeast
1	teaspoon sugar
³/₄	cup warm water
1¹/₂	cups sifted flour
1¹/₄	cups semolina flour
1	teaspoon salt

TOPPINGS

Olive oil and herbs
Thinly sliced tomatoes, mozzarella, and rosemary
Black olives and fresh tomato sauce
Smoked salmon and chèvre
Parmesan, tomato sauce, and thyme
Anchovies, olive oil, and capers
Garlic, thinly sliced yellow tomatoes, and olive oil
Clams, olive oil, and Parmesan cheese
Pumate tomatoes and mozzarella cheese
Flat leaf parsley, fresh tomato sauce, and mozzarella

Dissolve the yeast and the sugar in ¹/₄ cup of water, and let it stand until the mixture starts to bubble, about 10 minutes.

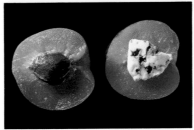

Top: *These miniature pizzas, made with tomatoes, black olives, and herbs, were baked on a cast-iron griddle in Kathy's Garland stove.* Left: *Fresh, halved apricots are topped with softened bleu de Bresse, a delightful French blue cheese.*

· · · · · · · · · · · ·

Combine the two flours and the salt in the bowl of a food processor. Turn on the machine and add the remaining water and the yeast mixture. Process until dough forms a ball. Put the dough on a lightly floured surface and knead for 15 minutes, until the dough is smooth and silky. Put the dough in an oiled bowl and let it rise, covered, for 1¹/₂ to 2 hours, or until doubled in bulk.

Preheat the oven to 400°.

Punch the dough down and divide it into small balls about 1¹/₂ inches in diameter. Roll each into circles of about 3 inches. Place on a baking sheet, cover with the topping of your choice, and bake for 8 to 10 minutes, or until the crust is brown and crisp.

Apricots with Bleu de Bresse

MAKES 30 HORS D'OEUVRES

¹/₂	pound bleu de Bresse, at room temperature
15	fresh apricots, pitted and halved

Spread 1 teaspoon softened cheese on each apricot half. Serve at room temperature, or put under the broiler for 1 minute, just until the cheese begins to melt.

VARIATION: Use halves of small ripe peaches or seckel pears.

Dried apricots can also be prepared this way.

CHAPTER FOUR

The Outdoor Barbecue

*T*he outdoor barbecue is a wonderful way to entertain. Even if one has just a terrace with a portable grill, or a deck outside the kitchen with a hibachi, nothing is as inviting as the smell of mesquite wood and grilling food. For a simple, practically all do-it-ahead hors d'oeuvre party, the barbecue with skewered foods is friendly, easy, and rather inexpensive. The party can almost be considered a meal if the menu is extensive enough.

The party we photographed was on the Mexican-tiled patio of Ruth and Paul Leserman in Beverly Hills. The party was held from 6:00 to 9:00 P.M. We served chilled beer, wine, and a few blender drinks made to order from fresh fruits and juices.

. . . .

Hors d'oeuvres for sixteen were served with style and ease from the brick grill in this terraced garden.

47

We arranged all the food on a glass-topped table, ready to be chosen and cooked by the guests. Clay dishes of various sizes and shapes held the skewered meats and vegetables, and small bowls held the sauces. The large fireplace grill—at convenient cooking height—was close to the table, so once each guest made a choice, it was very easy to grill it quickly. As at most outdoor parties, one guest offered his services as barbecue chef, making the other guests' tasks even simpler.

We used long bamboo skewers. Since the meat is cut into bite-size pieces for hors d'oeuvres, the bamboo is sturdy enough to use, because the skewer stays on the grill only a few minutes. (Soak the bamboo skewers in water for an hour to make them more flame-retardant.) For main-course grilling, metal skewers are better, because they will not burn up if left on the fire.

The main secret to a successful barbecue is in flavorful marinades and basting sauces for the meats and vegetables. We used quite a variety of meats and marinated each with a different combination of herbs, spices, oils, and vinegars. The vegetables were basted during grilling with flavored herb butters. Parsley and rosemary ''brushes'' were fashioned onto wooden chopsticks with twine and used to baste the skewers as they grilled.

We prepared three of each type of meat skewer per guest. The meats were cut up the day before the party and marinated in the refrigerator overnight. The vegetables were prepared the morning of the party. Baby pork ribs and chicken wings were marinated overnight. Most of the fruit for the drinks was purchased several days before the party—pineapples were ripened, mangoes and bananas softened. Only the strawberries were purchased the day of the party. Ice cubes were made in quantity and bagged ahead of time. Wine and beer were chilled in the basement refrigerator. Several hours before the party, two of us skewered all the meats, vegetables, and fruits and arranged them in clay dishes. Leftover marinade was poured over the skewers, and the dishes were covered and refrigerated until the time of the party. The fruit for the drinks was cut up several hours before the party and kept chilled. A half hour before the guests arrived, the fire was lit and the glasses were put out.

—>>> <<<—

Menu

for Sixteen

BLACKENED LEEKS · SKEWERED OKRA

GRILLED EGGPLANT · BARBECUED BEEF STRIPS

LAMB AND EGGPLANT SKEWERS · CHICKEN AND PEPPER SKEWERS

PORK AND MANGO SKEWERS · CHICKEN WING ''LEGS''

VEAL AND PEARL ONION SKEWERS · COCKTAIL RIBS

BARBECUED CHICKEN WINGS · GRILLED SAUSAGES

FRESH FRUIT DAIQUIRIS

PIÑA COLADAS

BEER · WINE

Cacti in clay pots were used as centerpieces for the tables. Brown glazed dishes and bags of fresh herbs, chili peppers, and spices are also stacked on the table awaiting use. We used colorful red and green bandannas as napkins.

. . . .

Blackened Leeks

MAKES 16 SERVINGS

**32   small leeks (about ¹/₂ to ³/₄
       inch in diameter), trimmed
       to 6 inches and washed**

SAGE BUTTER
MAKES ¹/₂ CUP

**¹/₄   pound (1 stick) unsalted
       butter
3   to 4 sprigs of sage, or
       1 teaspoon crumbled
       dried sage
¹/₄   teaspoon freshly grated
       nutmeg**

Blanch the leeks in boiling water
for 3 to 4 minutes. Drain.

Melt the butter with the sage and
nutmeg.

Grill the leeks over hot coals for 6 to
7 minutes, basting with the sage
butter two or three times. Turn the
leeks with metal tongs so that the
exteriors are evenly charred.

NOTE: Although we did not skewer the leeks, you could put them on
8-inch skewers to grill.

⇛⤜

Skewered Okra

MAKES 16 SKEWERS

**32   firm, fresh baby okra pods
       (2 to 3 inches long)**

THYME BUTTER
MAKES ¹/₂ CUP

**¹/₄   pound (1 stick) unsalted
       butter
3   to 4 sprigs of fresh thyme,
       or ¹/₂ teaspoon dried
       thyme
¹/₂   teaspoon ground cumin**

Blanche the okra for 3 minutes in
boiling water. Drain and put 2 okra
pods on each 6-inch skewer.

Melt the butter with thyme and
cumin.

Grill the okra over hot coals until
slightly browned, about 6 to 7 minutes, brushing two or three times
with thyme butter.

Grilled Eggplant

MAKES 16 SKEWERS

CORIANDER BUTTER
MAKES ½ CUP

- ¼ pound (1 stick) unsalted butter
- 1 tablespoon chopped fresh coriander
- 1 tablespoon lime juice
- 1 garlic clove, minced
- ¼ teaspoon hot pepper flakes

- 2 long, light purple Japanese eggplants, cut diagonally into ½-inch slices

Melt the butter with coriander, lime juice, garlic, and hot pepper flakes.

Put 1 eggplant slice on each 6-inch bamboo skewer (run the skewer through the diameter of the eggplant slice so it holds while cooking) and grill over hot coals for 6 to 7 minutes, basting two or three times with coriander butter, until eggplant is charred.

NOTE: Since the Japanese eggplant we used is quite sweet, it does not need to be salted. However, most other varieties of eggplant require an advance sprinkling with salt. Using 1 tablespoon per pound of cut eggplant, let the eggplant sit for about an hour, rinse, and pat dry. Grill as above.

VARIATION: Skewer 1 large shitake or Black Forest mushroom cap and grill, basting with coriander butter.

->>>«<-

Barbecued Beef Strips

MAKES 30 SKEWERS

- 2 pounds flank steak
- 1 medium yellow onion, peeled and thinly sliced
- 2 bay leaves, crushed
- 10 whole black peppercorns
- 1 cup red wine
- ⅓ cup olive oil
- 1 small bunch of Italian parsley
- 3 to 4 sprigs of thyme
  Salt and freshly ground black pepper to taste

Cut the steak crosswise at a 45-degree angle to make the strips 1 inch × ⅛ inch × 5 to 6 inches wide. Set aside.

Combine the remaining ingredients in a large mixing bowl, add the steak strips, and marinate overnight in a refrigerator.

To skewer, weave an 8-inch bamboo skewer through each strip of meat.

Place the skewers over hot coals and grill for 4 to 5 minutes, turning once. Serve immediately.

· · · · · · · · · · · ·

The patio had several large glass-topped tables, and the largest was used to display the skewered foods before they were cooked. Guests served themselves from this table and then grilled their choices over a mesquite fire. Below: Strips of flank steak are marinated in a mixture of olive oil, wine, and herbs, skewered, and grilled.

Veal and Pearl Onion Skewers

MAKES 40 TO 50 SKEWERS

- 1/2 cup olive oil
- 3 tablespoons white wine vinegar
- 3 tablespoons white wine
- 1/4 cup capers
- 1/4 cup chopped chervil or parsley
- 2 pounds veal, cut into 3/4-inch cubes
- 2 pints red or white pearl onions, peeled

Combine the oil, vinegar, wine, capers, and chervil in a mixing bowl. Add the meat and marinate overnight.

Arrange the meat and onions on the skewers, 2 pieces of meat and 1 onion per skewer.

Grill over hot charcoal for 4 to 5 minutes, turning once. Serve hot.

. . . .

Below left: *Chunks of marinated veal are skewered with red pearl onions.* Below right: *Grilled lamb and Japanese eggplant slices arranged in an earthenware pie dish.*

Lamb and Eggplant Skewers

MAKES 30 TO 40 SKEWERS

- 1/2 cup olive oil
- 1/4 cup sherry vinegar
- 1/4 cup sherry
- 1 garlic clove, crushed
- 1 tablespoon soy sauce
- 1 1/2 pounds lamb, cut into 3/4-inch cubes
- 4 Japanese eggplants, sliced 1/2-inch thick on the diagonal

Combine the olive oil, vinegar, sherry, garlic, and soy sauce in a mixing bowl. Add the lamb and marinate it overnight.

Arrange the lamb and eggplant on the skewers, 2 pieces of meat and 1 piece of eggplant per skewer.

Cook over hot charcoal for 4 to 5 minutes, turning once. Serve hot.

NOTE: Use any variety of eggplant if the more tender Japanese eggplants are not available. Just remember to place the cubed or sliced eggplant in a colander, sprinkle with 2 teaspoons salt, and let drain for 2 hours.

Chicken and Pepper Skewers

MAKES 50 SKEWERS

- 1/2 cup olive oil
- 3 tablespoons soy sauce
- 1/4 cup rice wine vinegar
- 1/2 cup sherry or port
- 1 bunch of parsley, chopped
- 3 whole chicken breasts, boned (about 3/4 pound each)
- 5 whole green or red bell peppers, seeded and cut into 3/4-inch cubes

DIPPING SAUCE

MAKES 1 1/2 CUPS

- 1 cup sherry
- 1/4 cup brown sugar
- 4 tablespoons soy sauce
- 3 tablespoons rice wine vinegar
- 3 scallions, chopped (white and green parts)

Combine the oil, soy sauce, vinegar, sherry, and parsley in a mixing bowl.

Skin the chicken breasts and cut into 3/4-inch cubes. Add to the mix-

ing bowl and marinate for 4 hours, or overnight.

Arrange the chicken and peppers on the skewers, 2 pieces of chicken and 1 or 2 pieces of pepper per skewer.

To make the dipping sauce, combine the sherry, sugar, soy sauce, and vinegar in a small saucepan. Cook over medium heat for 20 minutes. Add the chopped scallions.

Grill over hot charcoal for 5 to 7 minutes, turning once. Serve hot with dipping sauce.

→≫≪←

Pork and Mango Skewers

MAKES 40 TO 50 SKEWERS

¾ cup hoisin sauce
3 tablespoons soy sauce
¼ cup rice wine vinegar
¼ cup olive oil
1 tablespoon grated fresh ginger
2 pounds pork, cut into ¾-inch cubes

3 mangoes, cut into ¾-inch cubes

Combine the hoisin sauce, soy sauce, vinegar, olive oil, and ginger in a mixing bowl. Add the pork cubes and marinate overnight.

Arrange the pork and mangoes on skewers, 2 pieces of pork and 1 piece of mango per skewer.

Cook over hot charcoal for 7 to 8 minutes, turning once.

→≫≪←

Chicken Wing "Legs"

MAKES 40 HORS D'OEUVRES

1 cup plum wine
¼ cup soy sauce
¼ cup molasses
2 tablespoons wine vinegar
2 scallions, minced
2 garlic cloves, minced
1 tablespoon grated fresh ginger
40 chicken wings (about 3½ pounds)

Combine the wine, soy sauce, molasses, vinegar, scallions, garlic,

and ginger in a large mixing bowl. Set aside.

Cut off the tips and middle portions of the wings. Use in stock or grill separately. With a sharp knife, loosen the meat around the middle joint and push the meat down gently, scraping the bone, to about three-fourths of the length. Turn the meat inside out around the big joint to form a drumstick.

Marinate the chicken wings for 4 or 5 hours, or overnight.

Grill the wing "legs" over hot coals for 8 to 10 minutes, until golden brown. Serve with Garlic-Soy Dipping Sauce (page 85).

· · · · · · · · · · · ·

Clockwise from left: *Ginger-flavored pork and pieces of mango are an interesting combination for grilling, and large individual caps of wild, meaty shitake mushrooms are perfect for basting with herb butter and grilling; skewers of chicken and red and green peppers are served on a bed of flat leaf parsley; chicken "legs" are actually made from a wing with the meat turned "inside out."*

Sausages are best when cooked slowly and evenly. Peppers are delicious grilled with the sausages.

. . . .

Cocktail Ribs

MAKES ABOUT 40 RIBS

 1   *slab lean, small pork spareribs (about 2 pounds)*
 2   *tablespoons olive oil*
 ½   *cup finely chopped onions*
 3   *garlic cloves, minced*
 1   *cup ketchup*
 ¼   *cup Dijon mustard*
 ¼   *cup cider vinegar*
 ¼   *cup Worcestershire sauce*
 ¼   *cup dark brown sugar*
 2   *tablespoons freshly ground black pepper*
 1   *tablespoon crushed red pepper flakes*
     Pinch of cayenne pepper
     Salt to taste

Have the butcher halve the spareribs horizontally, then cut into individual ribs.

Heat the olive oil in a large skillet over low heat. Sauté the onions and garlic for 5 minutes. Add the ketchup, mustard, vinegar, Worcestershire sauce, sugar, black and red pepper, and cayenne pepper, and cook for 20 to 30 minutes. Season with salt.

Pour the mixture over the ribs and marinate for 3 or 4 hours or overnight. Grill over hot coals for 12 to 15 minutes.

→⋙⋘←

Barbecued Chicken Wings

MAKES 40 HORS D'OEUVRES

 ½   *cup olive oil*
 ½   *cup chopped onions*
 1   *cup water*
 ½   *cup wine vinegar*
 3   *tablespoons Worcestershire sauce*
 ½   *cup lemon juice*
 4   *tablespoons brown sugar*
 2   *cups ketchup*
 1   *tablespoon paprika*
     Salt and freshly ground black pepper to taste
 40 *chicken wings (about 3½ pounds)*

Heat the olive oil in a large skillet

over a medium-high flame and sauté the onions for 5 minutes, or until soft. Add all remaining ingredients except the chicken wings. Bring to a simmer and cook over medium-low heat for 20 minutes. Remove the pan from the heat and let the mixture cool completely.

Put the chicken wings in a bowl, pour the barbecue sauce over them, and marinate for 24 to 48 hours in the refrigerator.

agonally or into short chunks for serving.

For the barbecue, we served the sausages cut into chunks on skewers. German bratwurst, bauernwurst, knockwurst, and weiswurst can be cooked on the grill with great results.

→》《←

Piña Colada

MAKES 1 DRINK

4   ounces unsweetened
     pineapple juice
2   to 3 ounces dark rum
2   to 3 tablespoons coconut
     cream
1   cup ice cubes

GARNISH
   Spears of fresh pineapple

Blend all ingredients in a blender at high speed until the mixture is frothy. Pour immediately into an iced goblet, garnish with pineapple, and serve.

→》《←

Daiquiri

MAKES 1 DRINK

$1/2$ cup freshly squeezed lime
       juice
3   ounces white rum
1   tablespoon sugar
       (or to taste)
1   cup ice cubes

Blend all ingredients in a blender at high speed until the mixture is frothy. Pour immediately into a chilled goblet and serve.

VARIATIONS: To make fresh fruit daiquiris, add any of the following before blending: $1/2$ ripe banana; 4 large, ripe strawberries; one ripe, peeled peach; one ripe, peeled apricot; or $1/3$-cup cubed mango.

Grill the wings over charcoal, basting often with the marinade, for about 20 minutes of slow and even cooking.

→》《←

Grilled Sausages

ALLOW 2 TO 3 PIECES PER PERSON

Many sausages, especially Spanish chorizo, Polish kielbasa, and Italian sweet or hot pork sausage, are delicious grilled over coals. I prefer spicy sausages cooked this way, and serve them with pieces of crusty buttered bread and assorted mustards.

Make sure the coals are hot but the fire is not flaming. Cook the sausages slowly, having pricked them with a fork to keep the skins from bursting. Cook them until crispy brown on the outside, and slice diagonally

THE OUTDOOR BARBECUE

CHAPTER FIVE

Champagne and Valentines

We try to do a wonderful party on Valentine's Day each year. Last year we catered a party at Henri Bendel's in New York, where a new fragrance line was being launched. Guests enjoyed a vast array of heart-shaped hors d'oeuvres, most of which were red or pink. Heart-shaped trays and boxes were filled with sugar heart candies and cookies, and myriad paper doilies accented the serving tables and bars. Heart-shaped ice cubes, tinted pink with crème de cassis, floated in tall goblets of chilled white wine or champagne.

This year we were asked to cater a very special party at one of New York's grandest residence apartment houses. The invitation to the party for fifty read, "Please come for Val-

. . . .

Heart toasts with salmon roe caviar and crème fraîche amid a collection of faience vegetable boxes.

57

entines and Champagne," giving no real indication of what was in store. The hosts allowed us to let our imaginations run free, and we came up with an elaborate, elegant, and quite substantial sweet and savory menu. We prepared all day at the apartment, amid the splendor of seventeenth- and eighteenth-century French antiques, clocks, and porcelains. From satin ribbons, fresh roses, tulips and other blooms, and antique paper valentines, we created tiny accents to remind everyone that it was a special day. The foods, too, were shaped into hearts; toast was cut with heart-shaped biscuit cutters, as were cucumber slices, black bread, cookies, and scones.

The foods served were rather expensive, but because this party was a substitute for dinner (it was called for 6:00 to 8:00 P.M.), the added expense of baby lamb chops, *foie gras de canard,* and large shrimps wrapped in bacon was relatively light.

All the hors d'oeuvres except the scones and blackberry butter were served by black-tie-attired waiters. Waiters passed tall flutes filled with champagne, goblets of Perrier, and sparkling kirs (champagne with cassis). The hostess provided us with French faience platters and French porcelain plates and trays, and it was on these that we arranged the food.

Because the apartment was so large, we used many smaller trays and plates for serving the food. That meant going back to the kitchen more often for refills, but the food looked and tasted fresher than if it had been arranged on larger trays. The hot hors d'oeuvres also were hotter, because they were served more quickly. Because the menu was rather extensive, we allowed two of each hors d'oeuvre per person.

There was no visible bar. Champagne and Perrier were chilled in the laundry-room sink, and a small table for glasses was set up in the family room to facilitate service. The family room was also used for decorating trays and as a return point for empty platters. The kitchen was very busy—grilled quail, grilled lamb chops, and sautéed foie gras require last-minute cooking and lots of attention, and three kitchen workers were very busy for the duration of the party (which lasted three and a half hours, not the indicated two).

→»«←

Menu
for Fifty

COEUR À LA CRÈME WITH CUCUMBER HEARTS
HEART-SHAPED TOAST WITH SALMON ROE CAVIAR · SAUTÉED FOIE GRAS
EGGPLANT CAVIAR ON FRENCH BREAD TOAST
GRILLED BONED QUAIL WITH CURRANT SAUCE
BABY LAMB CHOPS WITH MINT SAUCE
GRILLED SHRIMP WRAPPED IN BACON · GRAVLAX WITH FENNEL
HEART SCONES WITH BLACKBERRY BUTTER
BROKEN HEART CHOCOLATE COOKIES
GINGERBREAD CUPIDS · SUGAR COOKIE HEARTS
SPARKLING KIRS · PERRIER
CHAMPAGNE

Coeur à la Crème with Cucumber Hearts

SERVES 60

This version of a coeur à la crème is made without sugar and flavored instead with dill, parsley, scallions, and white pepper. We served the coeur on a lacquered mahogany tray surrounded by sliced cucumbers that had been cut into heart shapes. Because the coeur was soft, the guests could easily scoop a bit of it with a cucumber heart, or spread it with a knife.

Porcelain or straw baskets in the shape of hearts are made especially for this coeur. The porcelain type has little holes in the bottom so that the whey can seep from the cheese mixture, leaving, a rich, dense concoction.

³⁄₄	**pound cottage cheese**
8	**ounces cream cheese**
¹⁄₂	**cup sour cream or Crème Fraîche (page 60)**
¹⁄₂	**cup heavy cream, whipped**
2	**tablespoons finely chopped fresh dill**
2	**tablespoons finely chopped fresh parsley**
2	**tablespoons finely chopped fresh chervil (optional)**
2	**tablespoons finely chopped fresh tarragon (optional)**
1	**small scallion, finely julienned into 1-inch lengths**
	Salt and white pepper to taste
3	**long, seedless cucumbers**

GARNISH
Dill sprigs

Combine the cottage cheese, cream cheese, and sour cream in the bowl of an electric mixer and mix with the flat beater attachment until smooth. Strain through a fine sieve two or three times. Fold in the whipped cream and herbs, and season to taste with salt and pepper.

Line a 3-cup heart mold (or several smaller ones) with three layers of cheesecloth, letting the cloth hang over the edges. Put sprigs of dill in the bottom of the mold and spoon in the cheese mixture, filling exactly to the top. Fold the cloth over the

An herb-flavored coeur à la crème is surrounded by heart-shaped cucumbers on an eighteenth-century English mahogany tray.

. . . .

cheese and set on a tray in the refrigerator for at least a day.

To prepare cucumbers, wash and slice each into rounds approximately ¹⁄₄ inch thick. Arrange the slices on a cutting board and, using a heart-shaped biscuit or cookie cutter slightly smaller in diameter than the cucumber slice, cut the slices into hearts. If they are not to be used immediately, put the hearts on a towel, cover with plastic wrap, and refrigerate. The cucumbers will keep approximately 3 hours before becoming limp.

To serve, unfold the cheesecloth, invert the mold onto a serving plate, and surround with hearts.

VARIATION: Use a fluted round biscuit cutter just slightly smaller than the cucumber and cut, leaving a bit of green around the edges.

Heart-shaped Toast with Salmon Roe Caviar

MAKES 50 TO 60 HORS D'OEUVRES

15   thin slices Pain de Mie
     (page 158) or good
     store-bought white bread,
     sliced very thin
7   ounces salmon roe caviar
     (large red eggs)
1/2 cup Crème Fraîche
     (recipe follows)

Cut the bread using a heart-shaped cookie or biscuit cutter small enough to yield 3 or 4 hearts per slice.

Put the hearts on a baking sheet and bake in a preheated 300° oven until dry but not colored, about 10 minutes, turning after 5 minutes so edges do not curl. Remove from the oven and let cool on a wire rack.

Whip the crème fraîche in a small mixing bowl until stiff and put in a pastry bag with a star tip.

When ready to assemble, spoon approximately 1/2 teaspoon salmon roe on each heart and top with a dot of crème fraîche.

→≫≪←

Crème Fraîche

MAKES 2 CUPS

2   tablespoons buttermilk or
     sour cream
2   cups heavy cream

Heat cream over low heat to 100°. Add buttermilk and mix well. Put in covered jar and let sit at room temperature for 6 to 8 hours. Refrigerate at least 24 hours before serving. The cream will become thick like sour cream.

NOTE: Crème fraîche can be kept refrigerated in a tightly covered jar for 2 to 3 weeks.

Sautéed Foie Gras

MAKES 40 TO 50 HORS D'OEUVRES

FOIE GRAS

2   cups milk
3/4 cup cognac (or port)
1   fresh duck liver
     (about 1 3/4 pounds)
1   teaspoon salt
     Large pinch of finely
     ground white pepper
12   to 15 slices Pain de Mie
     (page 158) or good white
     bread, sliced very thin

CHIVE TOPPING

1/4 cup olive oil
1   tablespoon balsamic
     vinegar
1   tablespoon fresh chives,
     cut 1 inch long
     Green or spring onions cut
     into very thin strips
     (optional)

CHANTERELLE TOPPING

2   ounces fresh chanterelle
     mushrooms, thinly sliced
     (Black Forest or small
     shitake will also do)
1   tablespoon unsalted butter
     White pepper and salt

To prepare the foie gras, combine the milk and half a cup of cognac in an earthenware or stainless steel bowl large enough to hold the liver. Soak the liver in the mixture overnight in the refrigerator, or for up to 2 days.

When ready to assemble the hors d'oeuvres, trim the crusts from the bread, using a long, sharp serrated knife, and stacking three or four slices at a time. Cut the slices into quarters diagonally to make four triangles. Toast as for Heart Toasts this page.

To make the chive topping, combine all ingredients in a small mixing bowl.

To make the chanterelle topping, sauté the mushrooms in the butter over high heat for 2 minutes. Season to taste.

Cut the foie gras into small, thin slices, 1/8 to 1/4 inch thick. Set a heavy sauté pan over high heat and sauté the slices 30 seconds on each side. Drain on paper towels and place on toasted triangles. Top with chive or chanterelle topping and serve immediately.

VARIATIONS: Foie gras can also be baked for serving. Remove the liver from the marinade and cut it in half at the connection of the two lobes. Remove any fat and tough membrane. Arrange the two lobes in a terrine (I prefer a rectangular one). Sprinkle with salt and pepper and douse with the remaining cognac. Bake in a preheated 275° oven for 15 minutes, uncovered. Turn off the oven and leave the terrine in it for 1 hour.

Remove the terrine from the oven and pour off the melted fat. Let the foie gras cool completely. Cover the terrine loosely with plastic wrap. Cut a piece of cardboard to the exact size of the terrine and place it on top of the plastic wrap. Put a weight (a jar or heavy bottle, for example) on top and refrigerate overnight. This will compress the liver and eliminate any excess fat.

Remove the weight and let the foie gras sit in the refrigerator for a day or two before slicing. (Foie gras will keep for up to a week in the refrigerator.)

Serve foie gras on French Bread Toast (page 63).

· · · · · · · · · · ·

Right: *An eighteenth-century lacquered Chinaman looks over small slices of sautéed foie de canard, served with a chive topping on a triangle of toasted pain de mie.*

Pink tea roses are mirrored in this Chinese export porcelain reproduction plate that holds tiny quartered grilled quail and a radicchio leaf of currant sauce.

. . . .

Grilled Boned Quail with Currant Sauce

MAKES 56 PORTIONS

14   quails (5 to 6 ounces each)
4   to 5 large sprigs of fresh thyme

CURRANT SAUCE
MAKES 2¹/₂ CUPS

¹/₂   quart chicken stock
     Bones reserved from quails

3   shallots, minced
4   tablespoons olive oil
¹/₂   cup sherry
¹/₂   cup red wine
¹/₄   cup currants or chopped golden raisins
     Freshly ground black pepper to taste
5   to 6 sprigs fresh thyme
³/₄   pound (3 sticks) unsalted butter, cut into small pieces
4   tablespoons (¹/₂ stick), unsalted butter
     Salt and freshly ground black pepper to taste

To bone the quails, lay each bird on its back and cut down the center of the breast along the rib cage, scraping the meat off the bone. Cut the meat from the backbone; you

should have two halves. Leave the wings intact.

Place the quail on the cutting board, meat side up. Halve by cutting through the meat where the breast and thigh separate. Remove the thighbone and reserve it for the currant sauce. Insert a small piece of fresh thyme under the skin of each quarter.

To make the currant sauce, reduce the chicken stock by half over high heat.

In another pan, sauté the bones and shallots in olive oil over medium heat until the bones are brown, about 8 minutes. Deglaze the pan with the sherry. Add the wine and reduced stock. Simmer for 20 to 30 minutes.

*Right: **A rare nineteenth-century Meissen ironstone plate holds delectably tender baby lamb chops, dressed with paper frills and served with a fresh mint sauce.***

. . . .

Strain the reduced liquid through cheesecloth and return it to the pan. Add currants, pepper, and thyme and cook for 10 minutes. Remove from heat and whisk in the butter, a piece at a time, until all is incorporated. If the sauce becomes too thick and cold, stir it over low heat for a second or two to warm it slightly. Do not heat it, or the emulsion will break down.

To cook the quail, melt 4 tablespoons butter in a pan over medium high heat and sauté the quail on each side until golden brown, 3 to 5 minutes total. Season to taste. Serve hot with currant sauce.

⇛⇚

Eggplant Caviar on French Bread Toast

MAKES 1 QUART, ENOUGH FOR 60 HORS D'OEUVRES

4 eggplants (about 4 pounds total)
¼ cup vegetable oil
⅓ cup soy sauce
¼ cup rice wine vinegar
3 teaspoons sugar
¼ cup finely grated fresh ginger root
¼ cup vegetable oil
¼ cup Oriental sesame oil
⅓ cup finely chopped cilantro leaves
4 scallions, finely chopped
   Hot pepper sauce to taste

1 to 2 loaves Homemade French Bread (page 159)—2-inch-diameter baguettes
   Light sesame oil

GARNISH
Fresh coriander, chives, or scallions

Preheat the oven to 350°.

Cut the eggplants in half lengthwise, brush all sides with vegetable oil, and lay face down in an oiled shallow pan. Roast until the eggplants collapse and are tender, about 45 minutes. Cool, saving the juices.

In a medium saucepan, heat soy sauce, vinegar, sugar, and 2 tablespoons ginger to boiling. Reduce the heat and add vegetable and sesame oil. Cook for 1 minute.

Scrape cooled eggplant from the skin and chop finely. Add the oil mixture to the eggplant, along with the remaining ingredients, and blend well. Season to taste, and refrigerate overnight to let flavors meld.

To make toast, preheat the oven to 325°. Slice the French bread into rounds or diagonal slices ¼ inch thick and arrange on a baking sheet in one layer. Brush each slice with sesame oil and bake until dry but not colored, about 10 minutes.

To serve, spoon eggplant mixture on toast and garnish each with a

fresh coriander leaf or a fine sliver of fresh chive or scallion.

NOTE: Cilantro is a green parsley-like herb with a pungent, very distinctive taste. Often used in both Chinese and Mexican cooking, cilantro is also called coriander or Chinese parsley.

⇛⇚

Baby Lamb Chops with Mint Sauce

MAKES 50 PORTIONS

50 very small, lean rib lamb chops
½ cup olive oil
4 tablespoons fresh rosemary leaves

MINT SAUCE
MAKES ¾ CUP

¼ cup brown sugar
4 tablespoons water
½ cup cider vinegar
½ cup apple jelly
½ cup fresh chopped mint

Buy the tiniest chops possible, and have the butcher trim the chops of all excess fat. Leave 2 to 3 inches of the bone.

Combine the olive oil and rosemary and marinate the chops in the mixture for 3 to 4 hours.

To make the mint sauce, combine the sugar, water, and vinegar in a small saucepan and cook over medium heat until reduced by one-third. Add the apple jelly and heat thoroughly. Just before serving, stir in the chopped mint.

Broil the chops or grill over hot coals or a hot cast iron grill pan for 2 to 3 minutes on each side. Serve immediately with the warm mint sauce.

Grilled Shrimp Wrapped in Bacon

MAKES 13 TO 15 HORS D'OEUVRES

- ½ cup olive oil
- 2 tablespoons champagne vinegar or good white wine vinegar
- 3 tablespoons chopped fresh dill
- 2 garlic cloves, minced
- 1 pound large shrimps (13 to 15 per pound), peeled and deveined, with tails intact
- 5 slices very lean bacon, sliced very thin

Combine the oil, vinegar, dill, and garlic in a bowl. Add the shrimps and marinate overnight.

Cut each slice of bacon into thirds and wrap a piece around each drained shrimp, securing well with a toothpick.

Grill over hot coals until the bacon is crisp and the shrimps are cooked through, 7 to 8 minutes. You can also grill them under a hot broiler, 4 minutes on each side, being careful not to burn the bacon or overcook the shrimps.

>>><<<

Gravlax with Fennel

MAKES 50 TO 60 PORTIONS

Traditionally, gravlax is a Scandinavian dish using fillets of fresh salmon, dill, salt, pepper, and sugar. In Paris I once tasted salmon marinated in fine olive oil, fresh fennel leaves, and black pepper. This is my version. I like to use a center cut portion of Norwegian salmon—it is fine-grained, pale in color, and delicately flavored.

- 1 3-pound piece of Norwegian salmon
- 1 cup coarsely chopped fresh fennel tops

Two nineteenth-century German dinner plates, adorned with roses tied with pale satin ribbons, display bacon-wrapped shrimp and a fennel-flavored gravlax on black bread hearts. The porcelain pea pods and leaf dish are eighteenth-century English ceramics.

. . . .

- ½ teaspoon coarse salt
- 1 tablespoon coarsely ground black pepper
- ½ cup light fine olive oil

MUSTARD SAUCE
MAKES ½ CUP

- 4 tablespoons Dijon mustard
- 1 teaspoon dry mustard
- 3 tablespoons sugar
- 2 tablespoons white vinegar
- ⅓ cup light vegetable oil
- 1 small bunch fresh dill, finely chopped

- 20 slices thinly sliced black bread or pumpernickel (the kind available in 1-pound loaves)
    Unsalted butter or Herb Butter (page 147), softened

GARNISH
Fresh dill (optional)

Have the fishmonger carefully fillet the salmon, leaving the skin on the fish. You can do this yourself using a very sharp fillet knife. Be sure to remove all fatty tissue from the fleshy side of the fillet—the marinade must penetrate throughout the fish. Any bones remaining in the fish can be removed with tweezers or needle-nose pliers when you slice the fish.

Put half of the salmon in a large glass dish, skin side down. Sprinkle with the fennel, salt, pepper, and olive oil. Place the other half directly on top and wrap well with plastic wrap. Refrigerate at least 3 days,

turning the fish twice a day and spooning the juices over it. After the first day, place another dish or tray on the fish and weight with a heavy pan or jar. This will compress the flesh, squeeze out any liquid, and create a finer-grained gravlax.

To make the mustard sauce, combine the mustards, sugar, and vinegar in a bowl or food processor. Add the oil drop by drop until the mixture is thick. Stir in the dill. Refrigerate until ready to use; the

sauce will keep up to 1 week.

No more than 2 to 3 hours before serving, put half of the fish on a cutting board. Scrape off the fennel and pepper. Cut the fish into 2-inch crosswise pieces, and with a very sharp, long knife, cut each 2-inch piece into very thin slices. Arrange them on sheets of plastic wrap, taking care to keep each slice separate. Refrigerate until ready to use.

Cut off the crusts of the bread if you plan to cut it into rectangular, triangular, or square shapes. If you are going to cut heart shapes, choose a cutter small enough so that you get at least 3 hearts per slice.

To serve, spread softened butter on each piece of bread. Top with thinly sliced gravlax and a dollop of mustard sauce. A sprig of fresh dill can be used as an additional garnish.

NOTE: When slicing, try to cut the fish into neat pieces that will completely cover the bread. I find rectangular-shaped bread best for this—3 rectangles cut from each slice of decrusted bread and the gravlax cut so that it is exactly the same size.

VARIATION: In place of the chopped fennel marinade, you can combine 1 cup chopped fresh dill, 2 tablespoons coarse salt, 2 tablespoons sugar, and 2 tablespoons coarsely ground black pepper for the marinade.

Heart Scones with Blackberry Butter

MAKES 40 HORS D'OEUVRES

BLACKBERRY BUTTER

½ **pound (2 sticks) unsalted butter, at room temperature**

½ **cup ripe blackberries, fresh or frozen (thawed and drained)**

40 **heart-shaped Currant Scones (page 22)**

In a food processor, process the butter and berries to a smooth purée. The butter will have a deep pink color. Spoon the butter into a small serving dish, and refrigerate until 1 hour before serving. Serve with a small butter spreader, to accompany scones.

VARIATIONS: Blackberries can be replaced by ½ cup sliced fresh strawberries, ½ cup fresh raspberries, ⅓ cup Damson plum preserves, or ⅓ cup raspberry preserves.

→»»«««

Broken Heart Chocolate Cookies

MAKES 35 TO 50
3- TO 4-INCH COOKIES

This is an adaptation of the Mexican Chocolate Icebox Cookie recipe found in Maida Heatter's Book of Great Chocolate Desserts. *We dribble melted chocolate over the tops of the baked cookies.*

¾ **pound (3 sticks) unsalted butter**

1¾ **cups sugar**

2 **eggs, lightly beaten**

3 **cups all-purpose flour**

1½ **cups best-quality cocoa**

¼ **teaspoon salt**

⅓ **teaspoon freshly ground black pepper**

A turquoise and yellow faience platter—my favorite in the collection—holds the egg-washed scones. I decorated the top of a wooden heart box holding blackberry butter with a paper doily.

· ·

⅛ **teaspoon cayenne pepper**

1 **teaspoon cinnamon**

4 **to 6 ounces semisweet chocolate, melted**

Cream together the butter and sugar in a large mixing bowl. Add the eggs and beat until fluffy. Sift the dry ingredients together. Stir them into the butter mixture and beat until well incorporated. If the mixture seems too soft, add up to ¼ cup more flour. Divide the dough into thirds and wrap in plastic wrap. Chill well, at least 1 hour.

Preheat the oven to 375°.

On a well-floured board, roll out the dough to ⅛ inch thick. Cut into hearts (or desired shapes) with cookie cutters and put them on a buttered or parchment-covered baking sheet. To make broken hearts, cut a zigzag through one side of each heart. While baking, the cookie will separate slightly and look just like a "broken heart." Bake for 8 to 10 minutes, or until crisp but not darkened. Let cool on racks.

When the cookies have cooled, drizzle some melted chocolate over each in a haphazard fashion. Let it harden completely before serving or storing.

≫≪

Sugar Cookie Hearts

MAKES 30 TO 40
4-INCH HEART COOKIES

½	pound (2 sticks) unsalted butter, at room temperature
1¾	cups sugar
2	eggs
3¾	to 4 cups sifted all-purpose flour
2	teaspoons baking powder
1	teaspoon salt
½	cup milk
1	teaspoon vanilla extract or cognac

ICING

MAKES ¾ CUP

1	cup (or more) sifted confectioners' sugar
1	egg white
3	to 4 drops of lemon juice Food coloring

Cream the butter and sugar in a mixing bowl until light and fluffy. Beat in the eggs, one at a time, until mixture is smooth and well incorporated.

Sift together the flour, baking powder, and salt. Add to the butter mixture alternately with the milk. Add the vanilla and mix until well combined. Wrap and chill the dough for at least 3 hours.

Preheat the oven to 375°.

Divide the dough into thirds and roll out each section to ⅛ inch thick. Cut the dough into hearts (or other shapes) with cookie cutters and place them on a buttered or parchment-covered baking sheet.

Bake until golden, about 8 minutes. Let cool on racks.

To make the icing, mix the sugar, egg white, and lemon juice in a bowl until smooth and creamy. You may need more sugar to reach the proper consistency; the icing should be like heavy cream. Add food coloring and put the icing in a pastry bag fitted with a small round tip, or in a paper cone. Decorate the cookies as desired by piping designs on them.

≫≪

Gingerbread Cupids

MAKES APPROXIMATELY
35 6-INCH-TALL COOKIES

For decorative cookies such as these, I prefer using the first rolling of the dough only. Scraps can be rolled a second time and cut into smaller shapes for less-important snacking.

½	pound (2 sticks) unsalted butter or margarine
¾	cup brown sugar, packed
2	eggs
4½	cups sifted unbleached flour
3	teaspoons ground ginger
1½	teaspoons cinnamon
1½	teaspoons baking soda
¾	teaspoon baking powder
½	teaspoon ground cloves
2	teaspoons salt
1½	cups molasses

Cream the butter and sugar in a mixing bowl until light and fluffy. Add the eggs, one at a time, beating until the mixture is smooth. Sift together the dry ingredients and gradually add them to the butter mixture, beating until well combined. Stir in the molasses and beat well. Divide the dough into quarters and wrap each in plastic wrap; chill for at least an hour.

Preheat the oven to 375°.

On a well-floured board, roll out

Valentine-shaped cookies are served from a marble-topped dresser. The clock, mirror, and candlesticks are all eighteenth-century French objects.

. . . .

each dough quarter to ⅛ inch thick. Using cookie cutters, cut the dough into desired shapes. Carefully place them on buttered baking sheets (you may need a large metal spatula for this). Bake 8 to 10 minutes, until the edges just begin to color. Let cool on racks.

≫≪

Sparkling Kirs

MAKES 1 DRINK

1	teaspoon imported crème de cassis (black currant liqueur)
8	ounces good-quality champagne or sparkling white wine

GARNISH
Rose petal or borage blossom

Pour cassis into a large bubble goblet. Add a couple of ice cubes, and pour champagne into the goblet over ice. Garnish with a rose petal or borage blossom and serve.

CHAPTER SIX

A Spring Wedding Reception

My favorite wedding receptions are those that adhere to tradition and have a feeling of simple elegance, restrained formality, and a friendly family atmosphere. I like best lovely finger foods served from trays by appropriately attired waiters or waitresses, music to fit the time and place and mood, lavish displays of wonderful flowers, and simple but generous bars serving good champagne, wines, and drinks. A reception need not be large to be fun and successful. Often a smaller party makes it possible to serve a greater variety of more unusual, expensive foods and better wines.

This particular wedding reception took place in the spring, although the menu is adaptable to almost any time of the year. Old and antique silver was borrowed from family and friends. White linens from the bride's collection were laundered and carefully ironed and used as drapes and table coverings. Cocktail napkins were an assortment of linen and voile lace-trimmed squares and rectangles, also from the bride's collection. The glasses used for all the drinks were old stemmed glassware that the bride and her sisters had accumulated. None of it was terribly valuable, but it certainly looked more personal and more delicate than the usual rental stemware.

Because the reception was for only twenty-four guests, the trays were on the small side and filled with only six or eight hors d'oeuvres. Only one kind of hors d'oeuvre was displayed on a tray, following my long-standing belief that the food looks better this way and does not stop conversation by posing a problem of choice for the guests when the tray is presented.

What helped make the presentation of each tray very special were the small bouquets of flowers and vegetables created for decoration. These posies can be used again and again and require little in the way of arranging. After each tray was passed, the posy was removed, the tray washed or wiped clean, the posy replaced, and new hors d'oeuvres were set out.

Some of the hors d'oeuvre trays were placed on a white-covered table, where guests could help themselves. Most of the hot hors d'oeuvres were passed on decorated trays, in an attempt to get the food to the guests before it cooled off. It is sometimes quite impossible to make sure the hot food is still hot when accepted by the guests, but it is easier when the number of guests is small. There were two people in the kitchen making hors d'oeuvres, filling trays, and replenishing the buffet table. One waiter passed hors d'oeuvres and another made and served drinks. Because it was a special occasion, four helpers was not excessive, even for a party of only twenty-four. Three experienced helpers could have managed, but it is difficult to ensure perfect service with fewer than four for twenty-four to thirty-six guests.

The menu was chosen by the bride and composed of hors d'oeuvres that she and the groom especially liked. The puffs, tartlet shells, barquette shells, and orange muffins were made days before the reception and frozen. The crêpe batter and fillings for the cherry tomatoes, cucumbers, and tartlets were made the day before the party. All that was left for the staff to do was to reheat the fillings and make the crêpes. Assembling all the hors d'oeuvres was a last-minute function of the kitchen helpers. It is best, where able, to make most of the hors d'oeuvres right before serving, ensuring perfect freshness and taste.

There were actually eleven different hors d'oeuvres served at this party, rather a large number in most people's estimation. But the party lasted three and a half hours, and the guests were quite satisfied by the time the cake was cut and served. The guests commented favorably on the great variety and were pleased that they did not have to go somewhere else for dinner.

Approximately three of each hors d'oeuvre were made per guest. When there are so many hors d'oeuvres to choose from, it is sometimes a good idea to vary quantities according to what the host thinks will be the most popular of the foods.

→>>«←

Menu
for Twenty-four

CRUDITÉS OF ASPARAGUS AND HARICOTS VERTS
CUCUMBER·ROUNDS WITH SMOKED SALMON MOUSSE
PEARS WITH GORGONZOLA
CHERRY TOMATOES FILLED WITH ARTICHOKES AND HEARTS OF PALM
ORIENTAL CHICKEN SALAD TARTLETS · BARQUETTES WITH LEEK CHIFFONADE
ORANGE MUFFINS WITH SMOKED TURKEY
PUFFS WITH CURRIED ONIONS
ROQUEFORT GRAPES · PUFF PASTRY STRAWS
PEAR-FILLED CRÊPES
WINE · CHAMPAGNE

A stemmed candy dish holds the crudité of thin asparagus and the long, tender green beans called haricot verts. The lemon-flavored dip is served from a small Revere bowl.

. . . .

Crudités of Asparagus and Haricots Verts

MAKES 60 HORS D'OEUVRES

2   **pounds pencil-thin asparagus**
2   **pounds haricots verts, stem end removed**

LEMON DIP

MAKES 1³/₄ CUPS

1¹/₂   *cups sour cream*
¹/₂   *cup ground almonds*
      Juice and grated zest of 1 lemon
      Salt and freshly ground black pepper to taste

Blanch the vegetables in large kettles of boiling water just until tender. The asparagus will take about 3 minutes and the haricots verts 2 to 4 minutes. Drain.

Immerse the cooked vegetables in ice water to chill. Drain well and refrigerate until ready to use. It is best to pack each vegetable separately, lining the dishes with paper towels or cotton dishclothes to absorb any excess moisture from the vegetables. Cover tightly with plastic wrap.

Mix all the ingredients for the dip and serve in a small bowl along with the crudités.

71

In a delicate contrast of colors, smoked salmon mousse is piped onto cucumber slices with a leaf tip, and garnished with a watercress leaf.

. . . .

Cucumber Rounds with Smoked Salmon Mousse

MAKES APPROXIMATELY
40 HORS D'OEUVRES

SMOKED SALMON MOUSSE
MAKES 1¼ CUPS

8   ounces cream cheese,
    at room temperature
2   ounces smoked salmon
    Few drops of lemon juice
2   to 3 tablespoons heavy
    cream
    White pepper to taste

2   seedless English cucumbers

GARNISH
    Watercress leaf (optional)

Combine the mousse ingredients in the bowl of a food processor and blend until the mixture is smooth. Chill at least 30 minutes.

Cut each cucumber crosswise into approximately 20 slices, each slightly less than ¼ inch thick. Cucumbers can also be peeled, striated with fork tines, or cut into decorative shapes with biscuit cutters.

Assemble hors d'oeuvres no more than an hour before serving by softening the mousse with a wooden spoon and putting it in a pastry bag with a leaf tip. Pipe mousse on top of each cucumber slice, and garnish with a small watercress leaf.

NOTE: If you prefer, you can slice the cucumbers a bit thicker than ¼ inch and make a small hollow for the filling in the center of the slice with a melon-ball scoop.

Topping Variations

HERB CHEESE (PAGE 143)

BLEU DE BRESSE
MAKES 1 CUP, ENOUGH FOR
40 CUCUMBER SLICES

4   ounces Bleu de Bresse,
    at room temperature
4   ounces cream cheese,
    at room temperature
2   to 3 tablespoons heavy
    cream

Put all the ingredients in a large mixing bowl or in the bowl of a food processor and blend until well combined and smooth. Place the mixture in a pastry bag and pipe onto the cucumber slices.

CRABMEAT SALAD
MAKES ABOUT 1½ CUPS, ENOUGH
FOR 40 CUCUMBER SLICES

1   6-ounce package of frozen
    snow crabmeat
⅓   cup mayonnaise

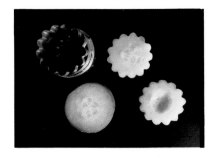

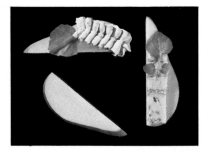

Cucumber slices can be prepared in a variety of ways. Biscuit cutters can vary the shape, and a melon-ball scoop can make a small hollow to hold the filling (above left). *Different pastry tips can also be used to change the look* (above center): *a star tip of salmon mousse, a rosette of herb cheese, and a leaf of trout mousse.* Above right: *A lengthwise slice of pear is the perfect foil for tangy Gorgonzola-Stilton, either sliced or softened and piped.*

. . . .

2   *tablespoons chopped fresh parsley*
½   *small Kirby cucumber, peeled and diced*
Salt and freshly ground black pepper to taste

Thaw and drain the crabmeat.

Put the mayonnaise, parsley, and cucumber in a mixing bowl. Add the drained crabmeat and stir well. Season with salt and pepper. Refrigerate until ready to use.

Spoon the crabmeat on top of the cucumber rounds.

PECAN CHICKEN SALAD

MAKES 1½ CUPS, ENOUGH FOR 40 CUCUMBER SLICES

1   *cup shredded cooked white chicken meat*
2   *teaspoons chopped fresh tarragon*
¼   *cup mayonnaise*
¼   *cup sour cream*
¼   *cup finely diced celery*
¼   *cup chopped pecans*
Salt and freshly ground black pepper to taste

Combine all the ingredients in a large mixing bowl. Spoon on top of the cucumber slices.

SMOKED TROUT MOUSSE

MAKES 50 TO 60 HORS D'OEUVRES

1   *8-ounce smoked trout (or smoked whitefish or mackerel)*
¼   *cup heavy cream*
Salt and freshly ground black pepper to taste
Lemon juice to taste
1   *to 2 tablespoons fresh or bottled grated horseradish*
2   *8-ounce packages of cream cheese, at room temperature*

Remove the skin and bones of the smoked trout and put the flesh in the bowl of a food processor. Chop the trout finely.

With the machine still running, add the cream in a steady stream. Season with salt and pepper, lemon juice, and horseradish.

Add the cream cheese to the trout mixture and blend until well combined and smooth. Press the mixture through a fine sieve, using a rubber spatula. Refrigerate until ready to use.

Pipe 1 tablespoon of mousse onto the center of each cucumber slice.

CURRIED TUNA SALAD

MAKES 40 HORS D'OEUVRES

1   *7-ounce can of tuna*
¼   *cup currants*
¼   *cup chopped toasted pecans*
½   *cup mayonnaise*
1   *tablespoon red wine vinegar*
2   *tablespoons chopped chutney*
Curry powder to taste
¼   *cup minced fresh parsley*

Drain the tuna well and put it in a mixing bowl. Add the remaining ingredients and mix well. Refrigerate until ready to use.

Spoon some of the mixture on top of each cucumber slice.

⇢»«⇠

Pears with Gorgonzola

MAKES 40 TO 50 HORS D'OEUVRES

5   *firm, slightly underripe pears*
¾   *pound Gorgonzola cheese*

GARNISH
Watercress

No more than 1 hour before serving, core the pears and cut in half lengthwise. Place each half cut side down and cut crosswise into slices ¼ inch thick. Spread Gorgonzola on the slices, and decorate each with a watercress leaf.

Cherry Tomatoes Filled with Artichokes and Hearts of Palm

See page 30.

→≫≪←

Oriental Chicken Salad Tartlets

MAKES 30 TARTLETS

ORIENTAL CHICKEN SALAD

MAKES 2$\frac{1}{2}$ CUPS

1$\frac{1}{2}$	pounds chicken breast
1	to 2 tablespoons soy sauce, to taste
1$\frac{1}{2}$	tablespoons sweet rice wine vinegar
$\frac{1}{4}$	cup peanut oil
$\frac{1}{4}$	cup vegetable oil
6	parsley sprigs, chopped
2	scallions (green and white part); minced
30	Tartlet Shells (page 150)

Cook the chicken breast in a 350° preheated oven for 20 to 30 minutes. Do not overcook. Let cool.

Skin and bone the chicken breast and cut it into $\frac{1}{4}$-inch cubes. Put the chopped meat in a mixing bowl.

Combine the soy sauce, vinegar, oils, parsley, and scallions. Pour over the chicken and stir well. Spoon into prepared tartlet shells.

Filling Variations

Crabmeat Salad (page 72)
Curried Onions (page 76)
Curried Tuna Salad (page 73)
Leek Chiffonade (page 76)
Pecan Chicken Salad (page 73)
Brie and fresh chopped herbs
Scrambled eggs and caviar
Scrambled eggs and chives
Shitake mushrooms sautéed with butter and parsley
Smoked mozzarella and sun-dried tomatoes (pumate)

. . . .

Below: *The unusual combination of hearts of palm and artichoke hearts is a tantalizing filling for cherry tomatoes, here held stationary by radicchio leaves.* Right: *Ultra-thin pastry shells can be filled with almost anything, including this Oriental-style chicken salad.*

Barquettes with Leek Chiffonade

MAKES 15 HORS D'OEUVRES

LEEK CHIFFONADE
MAKES 1 CUP

2	medium-size leeks, trimmed and washed
4	tablespoons (½ stick) unsalted butter
1	tablespoon finely chopped fennel top
⅓	cup Crème Fraîche (page 60) Salt and freshly ground black pepper to taste
15	Barquette Shells (page 150)

To make the chiffonade, slice the leeks crosswise very thinly.

Heat the butter in a small saucepan over a medium-low flame. Cook the leeks for about 10 minutes, or until soft. Do not let them brown.

Add the fennel, crème fraîche, and salt and pepper.

Bring to a simmer. Remove from the heat. Fill barquettes with the warm mixture and serve.

NOTE: The leek mixture can be made ahead, refrigerated, and re-heated over simmering water.

→»«←

Puffs with Curried Onions

MAKES 40 TO 50 HORS D'OEUVRES

CURRIED ONIONS
MAKES 1½ CUPS

6	tablespoons (¾ stick) unsalted butter
4	large onions, peeled and finely chopped Salt and freshly ground black pepper to taste
1	tablespoon flour
2	to 3 teaspoons curry powder, or to taste
¾	cup heavy cream
40	Pâte à Choux Puffs (page 150)

Heat 3 tablespoons of the butter in a small skillet and sauté the onions until transluscent. Season with salt and pepper. Melt the remaining butter in a saucepan over medium heat. Add the flour and cook for 3 to 4 minutes, stirring constantly. Add the curry powder and cream. Cook, stirring constantly, until smooth, about 5 minutes. Add the onion mixture. If the sauce is too thick, thin it with a little more cream. Check for seasoning.

Immediately before serving, spoon warm filling into pâte à choux puffs.

→»«←

Orange Muffins with Smoked Turkey

MAKES 30 HORS D'OEUVRES

ORANGE MUFFINS
MAKES 30 SMALL MUFFINS

1	cup sugar
½	cup (1 stick) unsalted butter
2	eggs
1	teaspoon baking soda
1	cup buttermilk
2	cups sifted all-purpose flour
½	teaspoon salt
1	cup raisins Zest and juice of 1 orange
½	cup sugar

• •

Below left: Boat-shaped pastry shells, called barquettes, are filled with a simple leek-and-crème fraîche concoction. Right: Pâte à choux puffs filled with curry-flavored onions.

½ **pound thinly sliced smoked turkey breast**
¾ **cup quince jelly**

To make the muffins, preheat the oven to 400° and butter small muffin tins.

With an electric mixer, cream the sugar and butter until smooth. Add the eggs and beat until fluffy.

Add the baking soda to the buttermilk.

Sift the flour and salt together, and add to the sugar-butter mixture alternately with the buttermilk. Stir until well mixed.

In a food processor, grind the raisins and orange zest. Add to the batter and combine. Spoon the batter into the prepared muffin tins and bake until golden brown and firm to the touch, about 12 minutes. Remove the tins to a baking rack and set close together. Brush the tops of the muffins with orange juice and sprinkle with ½ cup sugar while still warm. After 5 minutes, turn out from pans. Let cool completely before cutting each muffin in half.

Cut the turkey into small pieces and put a small amount on each muffin bottom. Top the turkey with ½ teaspoon quince jelly, cover with muffin top, and serve.

Variations

Corn Muffins (page 124) with smoked turkey and quince jelly
Orange Muffins with slivers of smoked ham and mustard
Orange Muffins with country ham and cranberry relish
Orange Muffins with Smoked Duck Breast (page 124) and plum jam
Orange Muffins with Fillet of Beef (page 146) and Horseradish Cream (page 147)

. . . .

A pierced candy dish was piled with a small pyramid of tiny orange muffins that we filled with sliced smoked turkey and quince jelly. Satin ribbons hold a small bouquet of roses and narcissus.

Right: *A true-to-life cluster of Roquefort grapes—a perennial favorite.* Below: *Blossoms adorn a bowl of puff pastry straws that we often pass with champagne at weddings.*

. . . .

Roquefort Grapes

MAKES 50 HORS D'OEUVRES

1	10-ounce package of almonds, pecans, or walnuts, toasted
1	8-ounce package of cream cheese
1/4	pound Roquefort cheese
2	tablespoons heavy cream
1	pound seedless grapes, red or green, washed and dried

To toast nuts, preheat the oven to 275°. Spread the nuts on a baking sheet and bake until toasted. Almonds should be a light golden color; pecans or walnuts should smell toasted but not burned.

Chop the toasted nuts coarsely in a food processor or by hand. Spread on a platter.

In the bowl of an electric mixer, combine the cream cheese, Roquefort, and cream and beat until smooth. Drop clean, dry grapes into the cheese mixture and gently stir by hand to coat them. Then roll the coated grapes in the toasted nuts and put on a tray lined with wax paper. Chill until ready to serve.

NOTE: Any leftover cheese mixture can be frozen and reused.

VARIATION: The cheese-coated grapes can also be rolled in chopped unroasted pistachio or macadamia nuts.

→>>‹‹←

Puff Pastry Straws

See page 114.

Left: *"Posies" of thin crêpes filled with cinnamon-flavored pears.*

. . . .

Pear-Filled Crêpes

MAKES 30 HORS D'OEUVRES

PEAR PRESERVES

6	pears
1	tablespoon sugar
½	teaspoon grated lemon peel
1	teaspoon ground cinnamon

2	ripe but firm pears (Bosc or Anjou)
30	3-inch Crêpes (page 155) Crème Fraîche (page 60) Cinnamon or freshly grated nutmeg (optional)

To make the preserves, peel, seed, and core the pears, and cook them with a small amount of water until very soft. Add sugar, lemon peel, and cinnamon. Blend well, and keep warm until ready to serve.

Cut each fresh pear in half and remove the core. Put cut side down on a cutting board and slice each half into long, thin slivers less than ⅛ inch thick. (Don't bother to peel the pears.)

To assemble crêpes, spread the crêpes out in one layer on a large baking sheet. Spoon a small amount of the preserves in the center of each, along with a sliver of fresh pear and ½ teaspoon crème fraîche. Fold crêpes or roll them into cornucopia shapes and arrange on trays to serve. Sprinkle with cinnamon or nutmeg.

NOTE: The crêpes can be made several hours before the party and kept well wrapped at room temperature until filling time. If you wish to make them further in advance, they can be frozen, and thawed in an oven right before assembling.

CHAPTER SEVEN

Oriental Cocktails in the Parlor

T his party was inspired by many that I have had in my own home. Andy and I have traveled to Japan, China, and elsewhere in the Orient, enthusiastically sampling the foods and flavors and drinks of those countries for many years. Although the foods themselves are fabulous, the presentation is also so exquisite, the porcelain and china are so interesting in shape and form and color, and the flower arrangements so thoughtful and decorous, that any party given with an Oriental theme is bound to be wonderful.

We served the food for this party in the parlor of our house. I gathered from cupboards and closets all the dishes that even faintly reminded me of the Far East. Exotic ingredients were collected from Chinatown in New York City, and from some local markets that carry Oriental vegetables and fruits.

Rice-paper cocktail napkins, bought in an Oriental market, were used during this party. The spareribs and the steamed dumplings are slightly messy, and soiling cloth napkins would have been embarrassing for the guests. Funny picks—some brass and bamboo, others silver—were used to pick up the mango and the melon balls.

The most unusual hors d'oeuvre, the sugar-tea smoked chicken, was taught to me not by a Chinese, but by an American sailor who had learned the recipe while stationed in China. The other recipes are adaptations of hors d'oeuvres that we have been cooking and serving at parties for several years. The spareribs are cut short, and only the meat is left on the bone, no fat at all. The rich marinade, sweet and tart, turns the ribs a deep dark glossy brown. The rectangular or triangular shrimp toast is everyone's favorite. It can be made in advance, frozen for a couple of weeks, and fried two

. . . .

A Peking duck stands guard over a table filled with Oriental-inspired finger foods.

81

or three hours before the party and reheated just before serving. The pearl balls can be made several weeks in advance, frozen, and steamed right before serving, but I find they are really best made the day of the party. If you make the dumplings ahead, freeze them. They can be steamed or fried in the frozen state with no real loss in their flavor. Smoking should be done several days before the party; the chicken actually tastes better after it has been refrigerated three to five days. The tea eggs can be made in advance and refrigerated in the tea liquid. Smoked shrimps retain the smoky flavor better if they are left in the shells and refrigerated in an airtight container. The spicy almonds are a crunchy, flavorful snack. They also make sought-after gifts, packed in little wooden boxes and tied with ribbons. The mango and melon balls can be prepared two or three hours in advance and refrigerated, well wrapped.

For thirty guests prepare two of each hors d'oeuvre per person. Our party took place before a local charity auction and provided our guests with sufficient food to tide them over until a late dinner. It lasted for almost two hours, although not everyone was there the whole time. Food was served from Oriental trays and platters, and most of it was arranged on two tables in the parlor. The smoked chicken, shrimp, and tea eggs were arranged on platters before the guests arrived. The spareribs, wontons, shrimp toast, and dipping sauces, were cooked and kept warm in the oven. Only the pearl balls and dumplings needed last-minute attention.

With a lot of before-the-party organization, a party for thirty seemed almost effortless. The use of a theme also spurred interest on the part of the guests, and they loved tasting the new and different hors d'oeuvres. Setting out all the food in only one room made it much simpler to replenish and refurbish the trays and platters. The bartender made it his job to pick up empty glasses in the other rooms, where the guests had found space to sit and talk. For a smaller group of people it would be thoughtful to provide very small plates so that guests could take more than just one hors d'oeuvre to another room. If an hors d'oeuvre buffet is your favorite way to serve cocktail food, I think it would be wise to invest in several dozen cocktail plates, small cocktail forks or picks, and an assortment of interesting, versatile trays on which to arrange this type of food.

→》《←

Menu
for Thirty

SPICY ALMONDS

CHINESE PEARL BALLS

TEA SMOKED EGGS WITH SESAME SALT · WONTONS

PLUM SAUCE · APRICOT DIPPING SAUCE · GARLIC-SOY DIPPING SAUCE

STEAMED DUMPLINGS · SHRIMP TOAST

ORIENTAL BABY RIBS · TEA SMOKED SHRIMP

SUGAR-TEA SMOKED CHICKEN

MANGOES · MINTED MELON BALLS

WINE

Spicy Almonds

MAKES 2 CUPS

3	tablespoons peanut oil
2	cups whole blanched almonds
½	cup sugar
1½	teaspoons salt
1½	teaspoons ground cumin
1	teaspoon hot pepper flakes
1	tablespoon sugar

Heat the oil in a heavy-bottomed frying pan over medium-high heat. Add the almonds and sprinkle the ½ cup sugar over them. Sauté until the almonds become golden brown and the sugar caramelizes.

Remove almonds from the pan and toss in a bowl with the salt, cumin, pepper flakes, and the remaining sugar.

Serve warm or at room temperature. Store in an airtight box or tin.

VARIATIONS: Walnuts and pecans can be treated in the same way, with excellent results. Also try cooked chickpeas or pumpkin seeds.

→≫≪←

Chinese Pearl Balls

MAKES APPROXIMATELY
36 HORS D'OEUVRES

¾	cup sweet or glutinous rice
6	dried Chinese mushrooms
1	pound lean pork, finely ground
1	egg, lightly beaten
1	tablespoon soy sauce
½	teaspoon sugar
1½	teaspoons finely minced ginger root
8	water chestnuts (fresh if possible), finely chopped
1	scallion, finely chopped

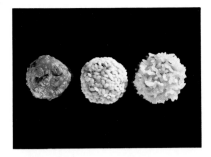

Left: *A ground pork mixture is coated with "sticky" glutinous rice, and steamed just before serving to make bite-size pearl balls. Below: A Japanese celadon and silver luster plate garnished with a single purple iris holds sweet and spicy almonds, an excellent accompaniment to cocktails.*

. . . .

Soak the rice in water to cover for 4 hours. Drain, pat dry, and set aside.

Soak the mushrooms in ½ cup warm water for 1 hour. Drain, and discard the stems. Chop the caps finely.

Mix together all ingredients, except the rice; blend well. (Your hands are best for this job.) Make balls 1 inch in diameter.

Spread the rice on a baking sheet. One at a time, roll the pearl balls in it, coating them completely. Set the balls on a baking sheet lined with wax paper. Refrigerate for up to 4 hours before steaming. (The balls can be frozen at this point for future cooking.)

Set a bamboo steamer in a pan or wok and add enough water to come to within 1 inch of the bottom of the steamer. Bring the water to a boil, put the balls on steamer racks, and cover and steam for 30 minutes. Serve hot.

Tea Smoked Eggs with Sesame Salt

MAKES 16 TO 32 PIECES

- **8** *eggs*
- **2** *tablespoons coarse salt*
- **4** *tablespoons dark soy sauce*
- **2** *whole star anise*
- **2** *tablespoons smoky tea (Earl Grey or Hu-Kwa)*

SESAME SALT

- **1** *tablespoon sesame seeds*
- **3** *tablespoons coarse salt*

Large pinch of freshly ground black pepper

Boil eggs 20 minutes over a low flame. Cool in cooking water. Drain the eggs, and tap the shells all over with the back of a spoon until each shell is completely crackled.

Return the eggs to the pan, cover with cold water, and add the salt, soy sauce, star anise, and tea. Bring to a boil, reduce the heat, and simmer very slowly for 2 to 3 hours. Turn off the flame and leave the eggs in the liquid for 8 hours.

Drain the eggs but leave in shells until ready to use. They keep well wrapped in the refrigerator for up to a week.

To make sesame salt, lightly toast sesame seeds in a hot frying pan, tossing gently over high heat. Combine toasted sesame seeds, salt, and pepper in a small mixing bowl. Set aside.

To serve, carefully peel the eggs. The whites will be marbled with dark lines. Cut the eggs into halves or quarters, and serve with sesame salt.

. . . .

Drain the crab, squeezing out as much moisture as possible. Put it in a mixing bowl and combine with the cream cheese, red pepper, water chestnuts, garlic, scallion, and black pepper. Refrigerate until ready to use.

Put 1 teaspoon of the filling in the center of each wonton wrapper, and fold as illustrated (right). Put the wontons on a baking sheet, cover with plastic wrap, and freeze until ready to use.

Heat the oil to 375° in a heavy skillet or a wok. Fry the wontons, a few at a time, until they are golden brown, about 2 minutes. Drain on paper towels and serve hot.

NOTE: Wontons can be fried ahead of time and reheated.

→»《←

Plum Sauce

MAKES ABOUT 1 CUP

1	cup plum preserves
1	garlic clove, peeled and crushed
3	tablespoons white wine
1	tablespoon Dijon mustard
1	teaspoon dry mustard

Mix all the ingredients in a small saucepan. Heat the mixture over a low flame, just to melt the preserves.

Serve with the fried wontons.

Apricot Dipping Sauce

MAKES 1 CUP

1	cup apricot preserves
1½	tablespoons grated fresh ginger
1	teaspoon Dijon mustard
1	tablespoon rice wine vinegar

Mix all the ingredients in a small saucepan and heat over a low flame to melt the preserves.

Serve with fried wontons, pearl balls, or spareribs.

→»《←

Garlic-Soy Dipping Sauce

MAKES ½ CUP

4	tablespoons soy sauce
3	tablespoons rice wine vinegar
2	tablespoons vegetable oil
1	teaspoon Oriental sesame oil (use half hot sesame oil if you wish)
1	teaspoon minced garlic
1	teaspoon minced scallion Pinch of sugar

Mix all the ingredients shortly before serving.

Serve as a dipping sauce for pearl balls, wontons, or dumplings.

Wontons

MAKES 50 WONTONS

1	6-ounce package of frozen snow crabmeat, thawed
4	ounces cream cheese, at room temperature
¼	red pepper, finely minced
4	water chestnuts, chopped
2	garlic cloves, minced
1	scallion, minced
¼	teaspoon freshly ground black pepper
1	16-ounce package of wonton skins Vegetable oil for frying

Right: *Oddly shaped Imari dishes mixed with majolica, celadon, and some Canton are wonderful serving pieces for* (clockwise from top right): *slices of sugar-tea smoked chicken, shrimp toast, tea-smoked shrimp, Oriental baby ribs, fried wontons, spicy almonds, mango, and steamed pearl balls.* Below: *Shrimp toast, made from thinly sliced white bread and fresh shrimp, can be made in square, rectangular, or triangular shapes.*

. . . .

Steamed Dumplings

MAKES APPROXIMATELY
36 DUMPLINGS

FILLING

- ½   *cup ground pork*
- ½   *cup ground chicken*
- ½   *cup chopped raw shrimps*
- 4   *tablespoons chopped fresh coriander*
- 2   *scallions, finely chopped*
- 2   *garlic cloves, finely minced*
- ½   *teaspoon freshly ground black pepper*
- 2   *teaspoons sugar*
- 2   *tablespoons soy sauce*
- 1   *teaspoon finely minced ginger root*
- 2   *tablespoons coconut cream*

- 1   *1-pound package of round wonton skins*
      Lettuce or Chinese cabbage leaves for steaming

DIPPING SAUCE

- 3   *tablespoons soy sauce*
- 3   *tablespoons rice wine vinegar*
- ½   *teaspoon hot sesame oil*
- 1   *scallion, finely chopped*

Mix together all filling ingredients.

Moisten one side of a wonton skin with cold water. Put 1 teaspoon filling in the center. Fold the wonton in half and crimp the edges closed. Put the wontons in a steamer lined with lettuce or Chinese cabbage leaves. Cover and steam for 15 minutes. (The leaves keep the delicate dumplings from sticking to the steamer.)

Combine the sauce ingredients and serve with warm dumplings.

VARIATION: Substitute ¾ cup lump crabmeat and ¾ cup chopped shrimp for the pork, chicken, and shrimp.

and process until the mixture is well combined.

Spread the shrimp mixture (approximately ¼ inch thick) on the strips of bread and dip the mixture-coated side in bread crumbs, covering well. Chill until ready to cook, shrimp side up on baking sheets. Cover with plastic wrap.

Heat oil 1½ to 2 inches deep in a large skillet. When hot (360°), fry toast on both sides until golden brown. Drain on paper towels and serve.

NOTE: Shrimp toast may be frozen, uncooked. Fry in hot oil as directed above, right from the freezer.

→»«←

Oriental Baby Ribs

MAKES 30 RIBS

MARINADE

- 2   garlic cloves, minced
- 1   tablespoon grated ginger root
- 2   teaspoons chili paste
- 3   tablespoons brown sugar
- ¼   cup molasses
- ½   cup hoisin sauce (available in Oriental groceries)
- ½   cup dark soy sauce
- ½   cup red currant jelly

- 30   small (3-inch long) individual pork ribs, trimmed of all fat

Mix together all the marinade ingredients. Pour over the ribs in a glass or stainless steel container and marinate for at least 8 hours, or overnight.

To cook ribs, preheat the oven to 375°. Put the ribs on a rack over a foil-lined baking sheet. Bake, turning often and basting with the remaining marinade, until the ribs are a dark golden brown, approximately 30 minutes. Serve hot or warm.

Shrimp Toast

MAKES 30 HORS D'OEUVRES

- 1   pound shrimps, peeled and deveined
- 1   medium onion, peeled and chopped
- 1   ½-inch slice of fresh ginger root, peeled and chopped
- ½   teaspoon salt
     Large pinch of freshly ground black pepper
- 2   egg whites

- 30   strips (1 × 3 inches) good thin-sliced bread, crusts removed
- ½   cup fine fresh bread crumbs (made in a food processor from bread crusts or trimmings)

     Light vegetable oil for frying

In a food processor or blender, process the shrimp, onion, ginger, salt, and pepper until finely chopped. With the motor running, drop the egg whites through the feed tube,

Tea Smoked Shrimp

MAKES 30 HORS D'OEUVRES

> **_Grated rind and juice of_**
> **_2 oranges_**
> 1   **_teaspoon salt_**
> 2   **_tablespoons rice wine_**
>   **_vinegar_**
> 30   **_large shrimps, unpeeled_**
> ½   **_cup loose tea, preferably_**
>   **_Hu-Kwa, Earl Grey,_**
>   **_or oolong_**
> ½   **_cup sugar_**
> 1   **_teaspoon cayenne pepper_**

Combine the orange rind and juice, salt, and vinegar in a mixing bowl. Add the shrimps and marinate them overnight.

To smoke the shrimps, line a heavy Dutch oven with aluminum foil. Sprinkle the tea, sugar, and cayenne pepper on the foil and set a rack over it. Cover the pot tightly and turn the flame to high. The sugar will melt, and the pot will start smoking. (Keep a kitchen exhaust fan going at all times to clear the smoke.) Turn off the flame, lay the shrimps on the rack, recover, and turn the flame to high. Smoke the shrimps for 5 or 6 minutes. Do not overcook, or the shrimps will become tough.

Cool the shrimps and keep refrigerated until ready to serve. Smoked shrimps will keep about a week refrigerated.

NOTE: If you own a smoker, the process can be altered to comply with the directions provided.

→≫≪←

Sugar-Tea Smoked Chicken

MAKES 12 TO 15 SERVINGS

> 1   **_roasting chicken (about 4½_**
>   **_pounds) or 3 Cornish hens_**
> 1   **_pound coarse salt_**
> 1   **_cup sugar_**
> 1   **_to 2 tablespoons smoky tea_**
>   **_(Lapsang Souchong or_**
>   **_Hu-Kwa)_**
> 3   **_star anise_**
> 1   **_to 2 tablespoons herbs_**
>   **_(optional)_**

. . . .

Below left: **_Large shrimp turn a rich mahogany color after smoking._** Right: **_Sugar-smoked chicken is quite delicate and flavorful and is best made several days before eating. It should be sliced very carefully so that each piece has a portion of the darkened skin_** (below right). **_I use a Japanese cleaver for slicing._**

Wash the chicken or hens and truss tightly with cotton twine or butcher string, folding the wing tips under the breasts. Fill the cavity with salt and put the chicken in a glass or stainless steel bowl that is just large enough to hold it. Pour on additional salt almost to cover. Cover the bowl with plastic wrap and refrigerate for 3 days. If you are doing more than one chicken, put all the chickens in the same bowl and cover with salt.

After 3 days, rinse the chicken under cold running water, making sure to rinse out all the salt in the cavity. Bring a large kettle of water to boil, immerse the chicken, and simmer for 20 minutes. (Simmer hens 10 to 12 minutes.) Drain well on a rack.

Line a very heavy roasting pan with aluminum foil. The pan *must* have a

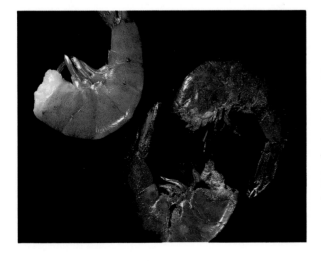

tight-fitting cover. Sprinkle the foil with the sugar, tea, star anise, and herbs (if desired). Set a rack inside the roaster over the sugar, and put the chicken on top. (If smoking more than one chicken or hen, do not crowd them in the pan.) Cover the pan tightly and put it over highest heat. Turn on the kitchen exhaust fan. Leave the pan over the flame for 30 minutes. Do not open the pan before the time is up. Turn off the flame and let the pot cool for 20 minutes. (Although a tight-fitting lid will help prevent the smoke from seeping out of the pan, you should plan to stay out of the kitchen during the time required to smoke the chicken; the smoke might become too strong.)

Remove the chicken from the pan, using tongs or a long fork. Be very careful not to break the skin. Drain the cavity over the sink and let the

. . . .

Fruit always seems an appropriate finale to an Oriental feast. The mango (below left) looks especially exotic when prepared in the traditional Eastern manner. A colorful melange of melon balls (below right) flavored with orange liqueur and fresh mint, is served with decorative toothpicks.

chicken cool on a rack. The skin will be a dark mahogany color.

To slice the chicken, carefully disjoint the wings and whole legs. Slice breast meat, always keeping a bit of skin on each slice. Slice meat from legs. Leave wings whole, to use as decoration. The chicken is best sliced 2 to 3 days after smoking and will keep up to a week, well wrapped in the refrigerator.

NOTE: Choose an old heavy steel or cast iron roasting pan for smoking. Once used, it is best reserved just for this purpose. To wash the pan, soak it in very hot water. Use just steel wool, no soap, to clean.

➤➤➤⫷⫷⫷

Mangoes

Generally, you would peel and cut a mango into chunks or simply eat it off the pit, getting lots of the fiber stuck in your teeth. If you prepare the mango this way, however, as they do in India and the Orient, you can avoid the fibers, and sticky hands as well.

Using a sharp stainless steel knife, slice each mango lengthwise into 2 pieces, avoiding the elongated pit in the center. Discard the pit. Score

the flesh of each half, making a fine crisscross pattern. Do not cut through the skin. Turn each mango half inside out, serve on platters with wedges of lime, and use spoons for scooping off the mango pieces.

➤➤➤⫷⫷⫷

Minted Melon Balls

MAKES ABOUT 40 BALLS

 *1   ripe but firm Spanish
      melon
  1   ripe but firm cantaloupe
 1/3 cup Mandarin Napoleon
      Brandy (orange-flavored)
      or Cointreau
 1/3 cup chopped fresh mint
      leaves*

Cut the melons in half. Scoop out all the seeds with a wooden spoon. Using a melon-ball scoop, cut as many balls from each melon as possible. Try to make the balls uniform and whole.

Add the brandy to the melon balls, stir well, and refrigerate until ready to use. Right before serving, sprinkle with mint. Serve from a bowl with small decorative picks.

CHAPTER EIGHT

Seafood at the Beach

I t is especially appropriate that this party was given at a beautiful house in Malibu overlooking the Pacific Ocean, because most of the fish and shellfish served came from that great body of water. This type of party is equally delicious, however, anywhere fresh, wonderful seafood is available. The day was warm but cloudy, and the fourteen guests were invited for an afternoon of tennis, horseback riding, swimming, and early cocktails. The grill on the deck of the main house, set high over the water on a cliff, and the hibachi on the porch of the beach cottage were the centers of activity.

As with the barbecue party, most of the food was prepared in advance. Fish was cut

. . . .

A driftwood fire and horseback riders provide a picturesque background for this party on the beach.

up and marinated in oils and herbs early in the morning, escabèche was made the day before, and goujonettes of sole (fried strips of sole) were readied early in the day and cooked just before serving. The green New Zealand mussels were steamed with shallots and white wine a couple of hours before the party, and the remaining shellfish was scrubbed and kept refrigerated until ready to pop onto the hibachi. Low tide was early in the day, and we were able to collect all types of seaweed, which we kept in buckets of fresh water for later use as table decorations.

We cooked the fish skewers on an unusual blue-and-white-tiled table grill, and arranged them on the hostess's collection of fish platters. The escabèche and goujonettes were served from platters on umbrella-shaded tables. Guests served themselves drinks. Cold beer, chilled wine, and assorted mineral waters were available at the bar in the main house, and from a galvanized tub, filled with ice, at the beach cottage.

The small beach cottage was down a very steep incline from the main house. For those guests who ventured down the path, green and black mussels, clams, dipping sauces and toppings, and whole Dungeness crabs awaited. With the aid of metal tongs, guests cooked the clams and black mussels themselves over the coals. The green mussels were served on the half shell. Chinese cleavers and wooden mallets were provided to make crab eating easier.

We allowed three or four of each hors d'oeuvre per person. The skewers used were bamboo, six, eight, and twelve inches long. Fish takes a very short time to grill, and the bamboo skewers, soaked in cold water first, were light, strong, and didn't burn up in the time it took to cook the fish. Vegetables that required little cooking, such as cherry tomatoes, were combined with fish that required only a short time to grill. The plump sea scallops were large and took longer to cook, so we put fennel on the skewers with them and tomatoes with the swordfish.

->>> <<<-

Menu

for Fourteen

GRILLED SWORDFISH WITH CHERRY TOMATOES AND FENNEL LEAVES

GRILLED SCALLOPS WITH CHERVIL AND FENNEL

GRILLED SALMON WITH THYME

GRILLED TIGER SHRIMP WITH DILL

GRILLED TUNA WITH BLACK PEPPER

ESCABÈCHE · GOUJONETTES OF SOLE

DUNGENESS CRABS WITH HERB MAYONNAISE

STEAMED GREEN MUSSELS

GRILLED CLAMS WITH BARBECUE SAUCE

STONE CRAB CLAWS WITH FOUR-PEPPER SAUCE

BEER · WINE · MINERAL WATER

Right: *Swordfish, here skewered with cherry tomatoes, is a firm, oily fish that cuts beautifully into squares for grilling.* Far right: *Cubed salmon steaks take only a minute to grill to perfection.* Below: *Very large, colorfully striped tiger shrimp.*

. . . .

Grilled Swordfish with Cherry Tomatoes and Fennel Leaves

MAKES 16 SKEWERS

> 1   pound fresh swordfish, cut into ³/₄-inch cubes
> ¹/₂   cup olive oil
> 2   tablespoons fresh fennel leaves
> 1   pint cherry tomatoes

Marinate the swordfish in the oil and fennel leaves for 2 to 3 hours.

Halve the cherry tomatoes and put on skewers with 1 or 2 pieces of fish. Grill over hot coals for 1 or 2 minutes, depending on the thickness of the fish. Serve immediately.

→»)«←

Grilled Scallops with Chervil and Fennel

MAKES 16 SKEWERS

> 1   pound sea scallops
> 1   fennel bulb, cut into ¹/₂-inch pieces
> ¹/₂   cup olive oil
> 3   tablespoons fresh chervil

Marinate the scallops and fennel in the olive oil and chervil for 3 to 4 hours.

Put 2 scallops and 1 piece of fennel on a skewer and grill over hot coals for 4 to 5 minutes. Serve immediately.

Grilled Salmon with Thyme

MAKES 16 SKEWERS

> 1   pound fresh salmon fillet, cut into ³/₄-inch cubes
> ¹/₂   cup olive oil
> 2   tablespoons fresh thyme
>
> Garlic-Soy Dipping Sauce (page 85)

Marinate the salmon in the olive oil and thyme for 2 to 3 hours.

Put 2 or 3 cubes of salmon on a skewer and grill over hot coals for 1 to 2 minutes, depending on the thickness of the fish. Serve immediately with dipping sauce.

Grilled Tiger Shrimp with Dill

MAKES 24 SKEWERS

> 1   pound tiger shrimps (12 per pound), or jumbo shrimp
> ¹/₂   cup olive oil
> 3   tablespoons chopped fresh dill

Peel, devein, and split each shrimp lengthwise. Marinate in the olive oil and dill for 2 to 3 hours.

Thread each shrimp half on a skewer and grill over hot coals for 2 to 3 minutes, depending on the thickness of the shrimp.

This unusual German-designed grill was used for cooking the skewered fish.

Grilled Tuna with Black Pepper

MAKES 16 SERVINGS

> 1   *pound fresh tuna,*
>   *cut into thin slices about*
>   *½ × ¼ × 1 inch thick*
> ½   *cup olive oil*

2   *teaspoons freshly ground black pepper*
    Dipping Sauce (page 105)

Marinate the tuna in olive oil and pepper for 2 to 3 hours.

Skewer and grill tuna slices over hot coals for no more than 1 minute. Serve immediately with dipping sauce.

Escabèche

MAKES 16 SERVINGS

> 2   *pounds fresh fish fillets*
>   *(sole, bass, or flounder)*
>   *Vegetable oil for frying*
> ½   *cup all-purpose flour*
> ½   *cup olive oil*
> 1   *carrot, thinly sliced*

1 large onion, thinly sliced
5 garlic cloves, peeled
1 cup white wine vinegar or champagne vinegar
½ cup water
3 to 4 sprigs of thyme
1 bay leaf
1 hot chili pepper, seeded and chopped
  Salt and freshly ground black pepper to taste

Cut fish into 2 × 1-inch pieces.

Heat the vegetable oil to 370°. Roll the fish pieces in the flour and fry until golden, about 3 to 4 minutes. Drain on paper towels.

Heat the olive oil in a skillet over medium-low heat. Sauté the carrot, onion, and garlic until soft but not brown, about 10 minutes.

Combine the remaining ingredients in a saucepan. Bring to a boil and simmer for 10 minutes.

Put the fish pieces and vegetables in a glass bowl, pour the hot liquid over them, and marinate in the refrigerator for 24 hours. Serve cold.

→》《←

Goujonettes of Sole

MAKES 16 SERVINGS

TARTAR SAUCE

MAKES ABOUT 1½ CUPS

2 tablespoons tarragon vinegar
1 teaspoon Dijon mustard
½ teaspoon salt
  Pinch of cayenne pepper
⅓ cup finely chopped cornichons (sour French gherkins)
1 tablespoon finely chopped shallots
1 teaspoon finely chopped capers
1 tablespoon finely chopped fresh parsley

Top: *Fresh, uncooked tuna is bright red. When grilled at home and served with a Japanese mustard dipping sauce, it is delicate and very tasty.* Center: *Escabèche is a colorful combination of filleted, quickly fried fish marinated in oil and vinegar with vegetables and herbs.* Bottom: *Goujonettes are thin strips of boneless fish, lightly coated with bread crumbs and deep fried. Serve with homemade tartar sauce.*

. . . .

1 cup Homemade Mayonnaise (page 20)
1 cup all-purpose flour
1 teaspoon salt
¼ teaspoon white pepper
1½ pounds fillet of sole
3 egg whites, lightly beaten
1 cup Japanese bread crumbs, or any bread crumbs made from good-quality white bread
  Vegetable oil for frying

To make the tartar sauce, combine the ingredients and refrigerate until ready to use, up to 2 days.

To prepare the goujonettes, sift the flour with the salt and pepper. Set aside.

Cut the sole into diagonal crosswise strips ½ inch wide. Roll them in the flour, then dip them in the frothy egg whites, and finally coat them with the bread crumbs.

Heat 3 inches of oil in a deep, heavy wok, to 360°. Quickly fry the strips of sole, a few at a time, until they are lightly golden, about 3 minutes. Drain on paper towels.

Serve goujonettes hot or warm, with tartar sauce.

NOTE: Japanese bread crumbs are available in Oriental markets. Each crumb is almost crystalline in shape, and they make a light, crunchy, and golden coating for fried foods.

95

Dungeness Crabs with Herb Mayonnaise

½ to 1 crab per person

In a deep, covered kettle, bring about 1 inch of water to a boil. Add the crabs (they should be crowded in the pot), cover, and cook about 7 minutes, shaking the kettle occasionally to ensure even cooking. After about 7 minutes, uncover the pot to see if the crabs have turned bright red; if not, cover again, and continue to cook, checking crabs every minute.

Remove cooked crabs from the heat, cool, and refrigerate until ready to use. The legs can be cracked and the back shell sliced ahead of time for easier eating.

Serve with herb mayonnaise.

→≫≪←

Herb Mayonnaise

MAKES 2½ CUPS

½   **pound spinach leaves**
2   **tablespoons chopped shallots**
¼   **cup watercress leaves**
¼   **cup chopped fresh parsley**
1   **to 2 tablespoons fresh tarragon leaves, to taste**
2½   **cups Homemade Mayonnaise (page 20)**

Put the spinach, shallots, watercress, parsley, and tarragon in a small pot, cover with boiling water, and cook for 1 minute. Drain and rinse under cold running water. Pat dry. Finely chop the mixture by hand or in a food processor, and stir into the mayonnaise. Refrigerate until ready to use.

Steamed Green Mussels

MAKES 16 SERVINGS

Green mussels are from New Zealand and Australia and are often available on the West Coast, and sometimes in the East.

4   **quarts green mussels (or black if green are unavailable)**
4   **shallots, peeled and finely minced**
4   **tablespoons (½ stick) unsalted butter**
2   **cups white wine**
3   **tablespoons finely chopped fresh parsley**

Scrub the mussels very well, removing any barnacles or beards.

In a deep, covered kettle, sauté the shallots in the butter. Add the wine and parsley and bring to a boil over high heat. Add the mussels, all at once. Cover and cook for 4 minutes, shaking the pot frequently to move the mussels around. Uncover the pot after 4 minutes to see if the mussels have opened. If not, cover again, and continue to check every minute. As soon as most of the mussels have opened, remove from the heat and pour the mussels and cooking liquid into a large bowl. Serve hot, warm, or cold.

VARIATIONS: Pour a rich, mustard vinaigrette over the steamed, drained mussels, serve in shells.

Remove one shell from the steamed mussels and serve with a bit of the cooking liquid spooned on top. Mussels on the half shell can also be served with a rémoulade sauce, Barbecue Sauce (page 98), or Black Bean Sauce (page 98).

. . . .

Steamed Dungeness crabs, littleneck clams, black mussels, and exotic green mussels from New Zealand.

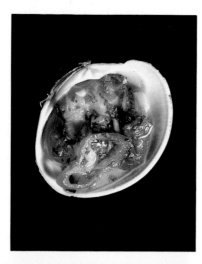

Grilled Clams with Barbecue Sauce

BARBECUE SAUCE

MAKES 1 CUP,
ENOUGH FOR 24 SHELLFISH

- 3 tablespoons olive oil
- 1 medium onion, minced
- 3 garlic cloves, minced
- 1 6-ounce can of tomato paste or 6 ounces good-quality ketchup
- ½ cup red or white wine
- ¼ cup cider vinegar
  Juice of 1 lemon
- ¼ cup honey
- ¼ cup Worcestershire sauce
- 2 tablespoons Dijon mustard
- 1 tablespoon hot sauce or Tabasco sauce, to taste
- ½ teaspoon ground cumin
- 1 bay leaf
  Salt and freshly ground black pepper to taste

- 3 small littleneck clams per person

To make the barbecue sauce, heat the olive oil in a saucepan over medium heat and sauté the onion and garlic until translucent but not brown, about 4 minutes. Add the remaining ingredients, stir well, and simmer for 20 minutes.

Grill the clams over hot coals until the shells open. While the clams are on the grill, it is best to use metal tongs to turn them. With heavy gloves or potholder mitts to protect your hands, pry off the top shells with a sharp knife. Top each clam with ½ teaspoon barbecue sauce, and serve hot.

NOTE: Besides being an excellent topping for the clams, this barbecue

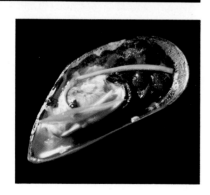

sauce can be used as a marinade for chicken or pork.

Topping Variations

CILANTRO SAUCE

MAKES ¾ CUP

- 1 bunch of cilantro, finely chopped (about ½ cup)
- 1 green chili pepper, seeded and finely chopped
- 1 tablespoon wine vinegar
- ½ cup vegetable oil

Combine all the ingredients in a bowl and serve.

TOMATO RED PEPPER SAUCE

MAKES 1 CUP

- 2 tablespoons (¼ stick) unsalted butter
- 2 sweet red bell peppers, roasted, seeded, and chopped
- 3 large red tomatoes, peeled, seeded, and chopped
- 1 teaspoon sweet paprika
- 1 teaspoon finely chopped fresh oregano
  Pinch of cayenne pepper
  Salt and freshly ground black pepper to taste

Melt the butter in a small skillet over medium heat. Add the red peppers and tomatoes and cook for about 5 minutes, until soft.

Add the rest of the ingredients and cook for 5 to 8 minutes, or until mixture is thick. Be careful not to burn the mixture. Serve with clams.

BLACK BEAN SAUCE

MAKES ¾ CUP

- 2 tablespoons Chinese salted black beans, rinsed of salt
- 1 tablespoon soy sauce
- 1 tablespoon sweet rice wine vinegar
- 1 tablespoon balsamic vinegar
- ½ cup vegetable oil

. . . .

Shellfish, always popular at any cocktail party, can be enhanced by different toppings. In addition to a spicy barbecue sauce, try grilled clams with a Mexican-style cilantro sauce (top), *or a zesty tomato-and-red pepper combination* (center). *Black bean sauce is a wonderful accompaniment to mussels* (bottom) *as well as clams and oysters.*

Combine all the ingredients in a mixing bowl until well blended.

Spoon a small amount of the mixture over cooked or raw clams, mussels, or oysters.

. . . .

Stone crab claws, full of sweet, succulent crabmeat, must be cracked before serving. For this party we arranged them on a huge earthenware platter around a bowl of spicy, flavorful, and very colorful sauce made with different types of peppers.

Stone Crab Claws with Four-Pepper Sauce

The stone crab claws can be purchased fully cooked and frozen. They must be thawed and cracked with a nutcracker or hammer before serving. Allow 2 to 3 per person.

FOUR-PEPPER SAUCE
MAKES 1 CUP

- 1   red bell pepper, seeded and finely chopped
- 1   yellow bell pepper, seeded and finely chopped
- 1   long green chili pepper, seeded and finely chopped
- 1   to 2 jalapeño peppers, seeded and finely chopped
- ¼   cup wine vinegar
- ⅓   cup olive oil
     Salt and freshly ground black pepper to taste
- ½   cup finely chopped cilantro
- ½   cup finely chopped Italian parsley

Combine all the ingredients in a bowl. Let stand 1 to 2 hours in the refrigerator. Serve with crab claws.

CHAPTER NINE

The Grand and Elegant Party

As a caterer, it is the grand and elegant cocktail party for hundreds that most interests me. Creating an atmosphere of beauty and fantasy, preparing thousands of perfect hors d'oeuvres, presenting so many hors d'oeuvres in a rather short period of time, and serving cocktails to so many presents a challenge that fascinates me time and again. It is at these grand affairs that we are able to utilize our new ideas, implement designs for decorations that would not work at most other locations, and staff a party as lavishly as the budget will allow. Not all these parties are extravagant in the amount of money expended; rather, they are extravagant in the use of creativity, decor that will interest and delight, and presentation of food-stuffs in quantities that often astonish.

Because these parties are for hundreds of guests, they are held at the most spacious, and often most peculiar, locations. In New York City a cocktail reception might be at the garden of the Cooper-Hewitt, the courtyard of the American wing of the Metropolitan Museum of Art, at the promenade in Lincoln Center, at the Park Avenue Armory, at the Passenger Terminal on the Hudson River, at the Bronx Botanical Garden, or in the Sheep Meadow in Central Park. One extraordinary party I catered was in the rotunda of the deserted United States Customs House on Bowling Green.

At these parties, a statement must be made, either by the decorations or by the food, or both. This cocktail reception was held at the aged but beautiful Burden Mansion on upper Fifth Avenue. The reception preceded a sit-down dinner for Paloma Picasso, who was introducing her new fragrance to New York. We commissioned two very large ice sculptures for the oyster bar carved in the shape of Paloma's perfume bottle. Oysters, served with Sevruga caviar, spicy crayfish, and blackish-green seaweed, decorated the oyster bar. Behind the oysters, a champagne bar was set up. Silver trays, each holding a dozen glasses, were filled with vintage Taittinger and passed to the guests by white-gloved waiters. The theme, if there was one, was red and black, so we attempted to create hors d'oeuvres that were red or black or a combination of both. Hors d'oeuvres were served on shiny black lacquer trays decorated with simple flowers and leaves. The menu was lavish; the hors d'oeuvres were as jewellike as we could make them.

Because a dinner was immediately following the reception, the number of hors d'oeuvres was kept small. Guests nibbled and drank for approximately one and a half hours. We had made three of each hors d'oeuvre per guest.

A large kitchen staff was necessary to create and arrange so many hors d'oeuvres in such a short time. There were just under two hundred guests and nine in staff in the kitchen making the hors d'oeuvres. Fifteen waiters served the trays of finger foods, and three more manned the oyster bar. The recipes for these finger foods are for smaller quantities (20 guests) than were actually served. However, the recipes can be doubled or tripled to accommodate the number of guests invited.

It is most important to realize that elegant, very large parties must be treated with even more intense care than smaller parties. The organization prior to the party is of the utmost importance, and the staff hired to execute the plans must be expert and quick. I find that by assigning one hors d'oeuvre to one or two people, they are made quickly and perfectly. Most receptions of large size last for one and a half to three hours at the most, and by delegating preparation in this way, everyone is most efficient. There should always be one person totally in charge of the kitchen, and one person, a party executive or captain, in charge of the serving staff and bartenders.

The setup of the party must be well thought out. Trays must be readied, decorations planned and arranged, all the beverages, wines, ice, and mixers ordered well in advance and on hand a day or two before the party, with the exception of the ice, of course, which is to be delivered two hours before the party. Rentals should be ordered as far in advance as possible, and delivered either the day before or early on the day of the party. All flowers and arrangements should be in place within one or two hours of party time.

→》《←

Menu
for Hundreds

CARPACCIO ON FRENCH BREAD

HEART TOASTS WITH BLACK AND RED CAVIAR

FOIE GRAS WITH BLACK FOREST MUSHROOMS ON FRENCH BREAD TOAST

BLINI WITH SOUR CREAM AND CAVIAR

TUNA SASHIMI WITH BLACK SEAWEED

CLAMS WITH GOLDEN CAVIAR AND ITALIAN PARSLEY

OYSTERS WITH SEVRUGA CAVIAR

Carpaccio on French Bread

MAKES 60 PORTIONS

60 ¼-inch slices Homemade
    French Bread, 1¾ inch in
    diameter (page 159)

CARPACCIO SAUCE

MAKES ABOUT 1½ CUPS

¼   cup white vinegar
12 cornichons (tiny sour
    French gherkins)
2   cups chopped parsley
2   garlic cloves
3   anchovy fillets

½   cup capers
3   tablespoons chopped
    onion
⅓   cup Dijon mustard
¾   cup olive oil

1   pound very lean top
    round, sliced no more
    than ¹⁄₁₆-inch thick
    Herb Butter (page 147)

Lay the ¼-inch slices of bread in a single layer on a baking sheet and bake in a preheated 300° oven until dry but not colored, about 10 minutes, turning once so edges do not curl. Remove from the oven and let cool.

To make the sauce, put all ingredients except the oil in a food processor and chop everything coarsely. With the machine running, add the oil, drop by drop, until mixture is creamy. Do not overmix. Put the sauce in a bowl, cover tightly, and refrigerate until ready to use.

To serve, butter the bread with herb butter. Place a small piece of meat on a piece of bread, and top with a little sauce. Cover the toast completely with meat; "ripple" the meat a bit for a nicer appearance.

VARIATIONS: Serve carpaccio on thin slices of toasted Pain de Mie (page 158) that have been spread with Herb Butter (page 147).

Cut the large pieces of top round into ½-inch strips and arrange zigzag on top of herb-buttered French bread. Dot with sauce.

→≫≪←

Heart Toasts with Black and Red Caviar

MAKES ABOUT
100 HORS D'OEUVRES

100 pieces of Heart-shaped
     Toast (page 60)
     Unsalted butter, at room
     temperature
7   ounces red caviar
7   ounces black Sevruga
     caviar

GARNISH

Whipped cream
Sour cream
Hard-boiled egg whites,
pressed through a coarse
metal strainer
Hard-boiled egg yolks,
pressed through a coarse
metal strainer
Minced white onion

Lightly butter one side of each heart toast. Spoon a ½ teaspoon of red caviar on one half and ½ teaspoon of black caviar on the other.

Top the heart with your choice of garnish.

. . . .

Above: *Carpaccio, or paper-thin raw beef, is rippled atop a slice of French bread and topped with a special sauce.* Left: *A black lacquer tray makes a dramatic service for elegant toasts of red and black caviar.*

Far left: *Sliced foie gras de canard with sautéed Black Forest mushrooms on French bread toasts.* Left: *Blini topped with sour cream and caviar.*

. . . .

Foie Gras with Black Forest Mushrooms on French Bread Toast

See page 60.

Above: *Two lacquer trays display tuna sashimi wrapped with seaweed and carpaccio.* Left: *Another lacquer tray of littleneck clams topped simply with a spoonful of golden caviar and flat leaf Italian parsley.*

. . . .

Blini with Sour Cream and Caviar

MAKES APPROXIMATELY
40 HORS D'OEUVRES

1	recipe (about 40) Blini (page 154)
3½	ounces red, golden, or black caviar
½	pint thick sour cream

Arrange the prepared, warm blini on a serving tray or platter. Put a few grains of caviar on top, and then a small dollop of sour cream. Serve immediately.

VARIATIONS: A strip of smoked salmon or a 2-inch tip of freshly steamed asparagus can be substituted for the caviar, if desired. A sprig of fresh dill is a perfect garnish for any of these combinations.

Crème Fraîche (page 60) may be used in place of sour cream.

Tuna Sashimi with Black Seaweed

MAKES 25 SASHIMI

1	pound fresh tuna fillet Japanese dried seaweed

DIPPING SAUCE

½	cup soy sauce
1	teaspoon prepared green mustard (wasabi)

Cut the tuna into uniform pieces 1½ inches by ¾ inch by ½ inch thick. Cut the Japanese seaweed with scissors into strips 1¾ inches by ¾ inch.

Wrap the pieces of fish with the seaweed and seal the end of the seaweed with a drop of water. Serve immediately with the dipping sauce.

To make the dipping sauce, combine the soy sauce with the green mustard.

NOTE: Wasabi mustard is available in Japanese markets.

→≫ ≪←

Clams with Golden Caviar and Italian Parsley

MAKES 60 TO 70 HORS D'OEUVRES

60	to 70 small littleneck clams (3 to 4 clams per person)
7	ounces golden caviar
1	bunch of Italian parsley

No longer than ½ hour before serving, open the clams and loosen them from their shells.

Arrange the clams on the half shell on a bed of crushed ice and top each with ½ teaspoon caviar. Garnish with the parsley leaves and serve immediately.

Right: *Iced oysters topped with a white-wine-and-shallot butter.*

. . . .

Oysters with Sevruga Caviar

MAKES 100 HORS D'OEUVRES

100 oysters (2 or 3 per person)
14 ounces Sevruga caviar
Lemon halves wrapped
in square of cheesecloth

No sooner than ½ hour before serving, open the oysters and loosen them from their shells.

Arrange the oysters on the half shell on a bed of crushed ice and top with ½ teaspoon caviar. Serve immediately with lemon halves.

VARIATIONS: You can also use golden caviar or other black caviar, such as Osetra or Beluga.

Oysters can also be topped with a few black sesame seeds and a sprig of fresh dill.

Topping Variations:

MAGENTA BUTTER
MAKES ½ CUP,
ENOUGH FOR 18 OYSTERS

2 tablespoons minced
shallots
½ cup red wine
½ teaspoon salt
1 tablespoon Balsamic
vinegar
¼ pound (1 stick) unsalted
butter, at room
temperature, cut into
small pieces

In a small saucepan combine the shallots, wine, salt, and vinegar. Bring to a boil and cook until the liquid has been reduced to about 2 tablespoons.

Remove the pan from the heat and cool slightly. The liquid should be warm enough to incorporate the butter but not hot enough to liquefy it.

Whisk the butter, a piece at a time, into the wine mixture until the mixture is well blended and creamy. If the mixture becomes too cool and the butter will not incorporate, return the pan to a low flame for a moment or two. Do not melt butter.

VARIATION: To make white wine butter, substitute white wine for the red wine and tarragon vinegar for Balsamic vinegar.

ORANGE BUTTER
MAKES ½ CUP

⅓ cup orange juice
1 tablespoon cider vinegar
¼ cup white wine
1 teaspoon grated
orange zest
¼ pound (1 stick) unsalted
butter

Follow the directions for Magenta Butter this page.

LEMON BUTTER
MAKES ½ CUP

Juice of 1 lemon
¼ cup white wine
1 teaspoon grated lemon zest
Salt to taste
¼ pound (1 stick) unsalted
butter

Follow the directions for Magenta Butter this page.

LIME BUTTER

MAKES ¹/₂ CUP

> *Juice of 1 lime*
> ¹/₄ *cup white wine*
> 1 *teaspoon grated lime zest*
> *Salt to taste*
> ¹/₄ *pound (1 stick) unsalted butter*

Follow the directions for Magenta Butter (page 106).

· · · · · · · · · · · ·

Top right: *Oysters with orange butter.* Center: *Iced oysters on the half shell with dill and sesame seeds.* Right: *Magenta butter turns its brilliant color from balsamic vinegar and red wine.* Far right: *Lime butter.*

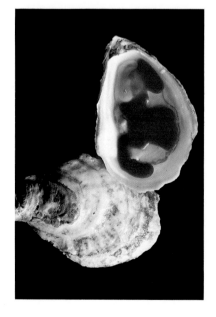

CHAPTER TEN

Antipasto Party in the Kitchen

This is one of my favorite hors d'oeuvres parties, because all the foods are so tasty, colorful, and fun to arrange. There is no service required other than an occasional refurbishing of the table or counter display. Most of the menu can be made way in advance, and the display set out one or two hours before guests arrive. The antipasto can be a party in itself or an informal, easy prelude to a dinner party. Because variety is very important in an arrangement of this kind, the larger a party you plan the better—the party pictured was for thirty-eight guests. It was held at the home of Lynne and Wayne Rogers, and the food was placed on a counter that divides the immense country kitchen from the family library. Small plates were available for taking food into other rooms, but most of the guests just helped themselves from the counter, coming back time and again to taste something else. An informal bar, composed only of wine and Italian mineral waters, was set alongside the antipasto, and guests helped themselves there, too.

Two unusual Bries were set on a large cutting board by the fireplace in the library. One was "en croûte," wrapped and tied in a casing of puff pastry; the other was glazed with a hard caramel coating and walnut halves. The baked Brie was cut into wedges and served warm. The caramel Brie was cut into small wedges and served with a crunchy piece of the caramel. The combination of sweet with the pungent Brie was unusual and very delicious. (This is a very nice cheese to serve at the end of a meal as a "dessert.")

Many of the items for the antipasto can be purchased at an Italian or Greek delicatessen or prepared at home. We prefer to make our own marinated vegetables, using fresh eggplants, mushrooms, peppers, artichokes, and string beans. The salamis were as numerous as we could find—it is less important to buy large quantities than it is to

108

find variety. Therefore, we purchased only one piece of each of the larger sausages and only two or three of the small. The cheeses were chosen as much for their interesting appearance as for the authenticity of their presence on such a buffet—several were French in origin, not Italian, but were of unusual shapes and textures and perfect for the display. We chose interesting olives and bought a pint or half-pint of each—Nyons, Niçoise, Moroccan, Greek Kalamata, Sicilian green, black, etc. Some of the blander olives were marinated in spicier dressings for a day.

We steamed the bunches of red, round radishes for 4 or 5 minutes, then immersed them in ice water for 1 or 2 minutes. Steaming makes the radishes tender, pale pink in color, and when chilled they are still somewhat crispy. The radishes can be marinated after steaming, but we served them just as they were.

The breads are the flatbreads of Tuscany called focaccia. We bake them with whatever toppings seem appropriate at the moment—rings of yellow onion, paper-thin slices of tomato and chunks of pumate (sun-dried tomatoes), sprigs of rosemary and coarse salt, salt and olive oil, oregano and garlic, or sage, olive oil, and coarse salt.

The hard-boiled eggs were peeled and cut into sixths and placed next to a mound of coarse salt. Quail eggs were hard-boiled but left intact, for the guests to peel right at the buffet. Small ornamental plates should be placed around the foods for olive pits, eggshells, and the like, and these should be emptied frequently during the party.

It is hard to determine how much of each item to provide for such a party. Although we allowed 3 shrimps per person, the vegetables were prepared in 1½- to 2-quart quantities, and the meats and cheeses chosen more by variety than by amount. Salamis and cheeses, if leftover, can be used for sandwiches or snacks; salamis and prosciutto actually last a long time when refrigerated. If caramel Brie is left over, merely scrape off the caramel, wipe the cheese clean with a damp towel, and refrigerate. Leftover Brie is excellent in omelettes or as quiche fillings.

→»«←

Menu
for Thirty-eight

WHOLE PROSCIUTTO · OLIVES
ROASTED AND MARINATED PEPPERS · ASSORTED SALAMIS
MARINATED BABY ARTICHOKE QUARTERS · MARINATED SHRIMP
SAUCISSON EN CROÛTE · STEAMED RED RADISHES
EGGPLANT SLICES SAUTÉED IN OLIVE OIL · HARICOTS VERTS
HARD-BOILED HEN AND QUAIL EGGS · MARINATED MUSHROOMS
ASSORTED ITALIAN AND FRENCH CHEESES
PUFF PASTRY STRAWS · FOCACCIA, ITALIAN BREADS
TUSCAN ARTICHOKE LEAVES · CRUDITÉ PICKLES
PAPAYA, MELON, OR MANGO WITH PROSCIUTTO
BRIE EN CROÛTE · RUTH LESERMAN'S CARAMEL BRIE
ASSORTED RED AND WHITE WINES · ITALIAN MINERAL WATERS

Old Japanese baskets lined with fresh herbs—rosemary, bay leaves, oregano, and basil—and white chicory hold a large assortment of salamis and olives.

· · · · · · · · · · · · ·

> 1 **lemon, thinly sliced**
> 16 **small black olives**

Steam the artichokes for 8 to 10 minutes, or until the heart is easily pierced with a knife. Cut each artichoke into quarters. Combine the vinegars, salt, pepper, garlic, lemon juice, and oils and pour over the artichokes. Add the bay leaves, lemon slices, and olives and toss well. Marinate 3 to 4 hours, or overnight.

VARIATION: If the artichokes are very young and tender, they can be quartered and marinated without steaming.

Two 14-ounce cans of drained artichoke hearts, or hearts of palm, can also be marinated as above.

→>> ≪≪-

Marinated Shrimp

MAKES 13 HORS D'OEUVRES

> 1 **pound jumbo shrimps (about 13 per pound), cooked**
> 2 **tablespoons tarragon vinegar**
> 1/2 **cup olive oil**
> 1/2 **cup vegetable oil**
> 3 **tablespoons chopped oregano**
> 1/2 **teaspoon of salt**
>   **Juice of 1/2 lemon**

GARNISH
> *Mache leaves*

Shell the cooked shrimps, leaving the tails on.

Combine the vinegar, oils, oregano, salt, and lemon juice in a mixing bowl. Toss in the shrimps and marinate for 3 to 4 hours.

Roasted and Marinated Peppers

SERVES 15 TO 20

> 6 **large bell peppers (red and yellow are best)**
> 1/2 **cup olive oil**
> 1 **garlic clove, finely minced Freshly ground black pepper to taste**

Place the peppers on top of a gas flame or under a broiler and roast them, turning often, until the skin is completely black.

Put the peppers in a paper or plastic bag or wrap them in paper towels and let them stand for 5 to 10 minutes. Rub off the skin, halve the peppers, seed them, and cut into strips.

Arrange the pepper strips in a shallow dish and sprinkle with olive oil, garlic, and pepper. Marinate for at least 4 hours, or overnight.

→>> ≪≪-

Marinated Baby Artichoke Quarters

MAKES 16 SERVINGS

> 8 **small fresh artichokes**
> 1 **tablespoon tarragon vinegar**
> 1 **tablespoon rice wine vinegar**
> 1 **teaspoon salt**
> 1 **teaspoon freshly ground black pepper**
> 1 **garlic clove, crushed Juice of 1/2 lemon**
> 1/4 **cup olive oil**
> 1/2 **cup vegetable oil**
> 8 **bay leaves**

Woven mats were used to cover the serving counter. This section of the buffet is indicative of the variety of foods offered: hard-boiled hen and quail eggs; salami; marinated mushrooms; twisted oil-and-red pepper marinated mozzarella; roast peppers; fried eggplant slices; and steamed haricot verts and radishes.

. . . .

Saucisson en Croûte

SERVES 18

BRIOCHE DOUGH

1   package of dry yeast or $^{1}/_{3}$ fresh cake yeast
1   tablespoon granulated sugar
$^{1}/_{4}$ cup lukewarm milk
7   tablespoons unsalted butter, at room temperature
2   large eggs
2   cups sifted all-purpose unbleached flour
$^{1}/_{2}$ teaspoon salt

2   to 2$^{1}/_{2}$ pounds French garlic sausage or Polish kielbasa (use straight sausage instead of a ring)
1   egg yolk
2   tablespoons heavy cream

To make the brioche, dissolve the yeast and sugar in the lukewarm milk.

Cream the butter with an electric mixer until smooth. Add the eggs and blend well. Stir in the yeast mixture. Gradually add the flour and salt, mixing until the dough forms a soft ball. This may be done by hand or in a food processor. Knead the dough for a few minutes, until soft and smooth but not sticky. Add more flour if necessary.

Put the dough in a buttered bowl and let rise, covered, for 2 to 3 hours, until it doubles in volume. Deflate the dough and let it rise again for 1$^{1}/_{2}$ to 2 hours. Punch down the dough again, and shape it into a ball and chill for 1 hour before using.

Prick the skin of the sausage with the tines of a fork.

In a pot large enough to hold the sausage, bring some water to a boil, reduce to a simmer, add the sausage, and poach for 30 minutes. Remove sausage and let cool. If using French sausage, remove the casing.

Roll the chilled dough into a rectangle 2 inches longer than the sausage and wide enough to wrap around it with 2 to 3 inches to spare. Place the cooled sausage in the center of the dough. Fold the edges and roll to encase the sausage completely. Seal with ice water and place on a baking sheet, seamside down. Chill for 1 hour before baking, or freeze to use later.

Preheat the oven to 400°.

Combine the egg yolk and cream and brush the brioche with the mixture. Score the top of the brioche with a sharp knife in a crisscross pattern, taking care not to cut all the way through the crust. Bake for 25 to 35 minutes, or until the brioche is puffy and golden brown. Cut into slices and serve warm or at room temperature.

VARIATIONS: Brush the sausage with a spicy mustard before encasing it in pastry.

Use Puff Pastry (page 158) instead of brioche.

Roll the brioche slightly larger and use some of the excess for crust decorations. Glue these on with ice water, chill, glaze, and bake.

➤➤❮❮❮

Steamed Red Radishes

MAKES ABOUT 20 RADISHES

2 bunches of small red radishes

Wash the radishes, leaving the leaves intact if they are crisp and fresh. If wilted, cut them off, keeping 2 inches of the stem. Leave the root end uncut.

Fill the bottom part of a steamer with an inch or two of water and bring to a boil. Steam the radishes for 3 to 5 minutes, depending on the size.

Remove the steamed radishes from heat and immerse in ice water to cool. Drain and refrigerate until serving.

➤➤❮❮❮

Eggplant Slices Sautéed in Olive Oil

MAKES 48 HORS D'OEUVRES

8 small, light purple Japanese eggplants
½ cup olive oil
   Coarse salt to taste
   Freshly ground black pepper to taste

Cut the eggplants diagonally into ½-inch-thick slices.

Heat some of the oil in a large skillet over a medium-high flame. Fry the eggplant slices for 2 to 3 minutes on each side, or until the edges become golden brown. Drain the eggplant on a rack, sprinkle with salt and pepper, and serve hot or at room temperature.

NOTE: Add more oil to the pan as you go along. Let each addition of oil get very hot before adding the eggplant.

➤➤❮❮❮

Haricot Verts

SERVES 38

2 pounds haricot verts

CREAMY GRAINY MUSTARD VINAIGRETTE
MAKES 1 CUP

3 tablespoons grainy mustard (such as Moutarde de Meaux)

3 tablespoons tarragon vinegar
½ cup olive oil
1 tablespoon chopped fresh tarragon leaves
   Salt and freshly ground black pepper to taste

Bring 8 quarts of water to a boil.

Blanch the haricot verts in the boiling water for 2 to 3 minutes. Remove them with a strainer and immerse in ice water to cool. Drain well.

To make the vinaigrette, mix all the ingredients in a mixing bowl until smooth and creamy.

Toss the drained haricot verts with the vinaigrette and serve.

➤➤❮❮❮

Hard-Boiled Hen and Quail Eggs

See page 24.

➤➤❮❮❮

Marinated Mushrooms

MAKES 12 TO 15 SERVINGS

1 pound medium or small mushrooms
2 tablespoons sherry vinegar
1 tablespoon balsamic vinegar
1 tablespoon freshly ground black pepper
½ cup olive oil
2 tablespoons small capers

Trim the stems of the mushrooms and wipe the caps clean with a damp towel.

Combine the vinegars, pepper, oil, and capers in a mixing bowl. Toss in the mushrooms and marinate for 3 hours, or overnight.

NOTE: If you use large mushrooms, quarter them.

Puff Pastry Straws

MAKES APPROXIMATELY
10 DOZEN 10-INCH STRAWS

1   *pound Puff Pastry*
   (page 158)
1/2 *cup poppy seeds*

Divide the pastry into three parts. Cover and refrigerate the pastry you are not using. Roll one portion of dough into a rectangle 1/8 inch thick and 10 inches wide. Sprinkle poppy seeds on pastry and press into the dough firmly, using a rolling pin.

With a pastry wheel (zigzag edges are nice), cut the pastry into strips 1/2 inch wide. Put strips on a water-sprayed or parchment-lined baking sheet and refrigerate until all pastry is used up.

Preheat oven to 400°.

Bake straws until puffed and lightly golden, about 8 to 10 minutes.

· ·

The flat Tuscan breads, called focaccia, and poppy seed puff pastry straws were homemade for this party.

VARIATIONS: Pastry can also be topped with 1/2 cup white sesame seeds, 1/2 cup finely grated Parmesan or Gruyère cheese, or a very light sprinkling of cayenne pepper.

Strips can be twisted before they are put on baking sheets.

➤➤❮❮

Focaccia

MAKES 2 10-INCH ROUND
FLATBREADS

4   *cups unbleached flour*
2/3 *fresh cake yeast dissolved*
   in 2/3 cup warm water
10 *tablespoons olive oil*
1/3 *cup water*
2 1/2 *teaspoons salt*

TOPPINGS

*Thinly sliced rounds of
yellow onion*

*Paper-thin crosswise slices
of tomatoes and chunks
of pumate (sun-dried
tomatoes)
Oregano leaves and
slivers of garlic
Coarse salt and olive oil
Rosemary sprigs, coarse
salt, and olive oil
Black olive halves and
coarse salt
Sage leaves, coarse salt,
and olive oil*

Mix 2 cups flour with the dissolved yeast. Knead the dough for 10 minutes, either by hand or in the bowl of an electric mixer with a dough hook. Shape the dough into a ball, and put in an oiled bowl to rise until doubled in bulk, about 3 hours.

Punch down, put the dough on a floured board, and knead again, incorporating the remaining flour, 1/3 cup olive oil, water, and salt. Knead until dough is smooth and elastic. Let rise again in a covered bowl for another 3 hours.

Preheat the oven to 400°.

Divide the dough in half and roll out on a well-floured board to circles or squares 1/2 inch thick. Brush with the remaining olive oil and press the topping of your choice into the top of each circle. Bake on a baking sheet until golden brown, about 20 minutes. Serve warm or at room temperature, cut into wedges, squares, or triangles.

NOTE: Slashes may be made in a decorative or random pattern in the breads before baking.

· · · · · · · · · · · ·

Right: *We bake focaccia with whatever topping seems appropriate at the moment. Fresh from the oven, this one is topped with paper-thin slices of tomato, oregano, salt, and chunks of pumate.*

Crudité Pickles

MAKES ENOUGH TO FILL 8 TO 10
QUART JARS OF LEFTOVER
CRUDITÉ VEGETABLES

4   *quarts cider vinegar*
3   *quarts water*
5   *cups sugar*
1/2   *cup pickling spices*
1/2   *cup mustard seeds*
4   *whole dried red chilies*
2   *tablespoons whole black
    peppercorns*

Combine all the ingredients in a large pot, bring to a boil, reduce the heat, and simmer for approximately 20 to 30 minutes.

Put the vegetables in a sterilized jar, pour the hot liquid over them, and seal. Store in a cool place for at least a week before using.

You can use almost any combination of vegetables and herbs. Listed below are a few suggestions:

YELLOW SQUASH

20   *small yellow squash,
     blanched*
8   *bay leaves*

RADISH

20   *small radishes, blanched*
2   *tablespoons pink
     peppercorns*
2   *tablespoons rose hips*

TURNIPS

10   *to 15 small turnips,
     blanched*
5   *to 6 dill sprigs*

YELLOW BEETS AND PEPPERS

10   *to 12 small yellow beets*
6   *to 7 small yellow peppers*

CARROTS

20   *small carrots, blanched*
5   *to 6 tarragon sprigs*

ASPARAGUS

20   *to 25 small asparagus
     spears, blanched*
10   *to 12 red pearl onions*

STRING BEANS

20   *to 30 small string beans or
     haricots verts*
2   *dried chili peppers*

OKRA

20   *small okra pods, blanched*
4   *garlic cloves, peeled*

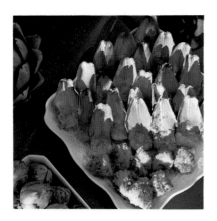

Heat ¾ inch olive oil in a heavy skillet. Dip pieces of the heart and the bottom half of each leaf into the beaten eggs, and then into the bread crumbs/cheese mixture. Sauté the leaves and artichoke hearts in the hot oil in one layer, turning once, until they become golden in color. Drain on paper towels and serve immediately.

NOTE: More oil may be needed for cooking. After each addition, be sure oil is sufficiently hot before sautéing more leaves.

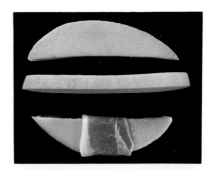

Opposite: *Crudité pickles are a perfect way to use leftover crudités and an interesting alternative to raw or blanched vegetables.* Above: *Tuscan artichoke leaves.*

. . . .

Tuscan Artichoke Leaves

MAKES 20 SERVINGS

Twenty years ago Andy and I were visiting Florence during Easter week. Our hostess prepared her version of artichokes for us; this is my adaptation of her very delicious creation.

3 large green artichokes
1 cup fresh bread crumbs
1 cup freshly grated Parmesan cheese
 Olive oil for sautéing
4 eggs, lightly beaten

Trim the prickly point from each artichoke leaf with scissors. Boil or steam the artichokes until the leaves are tender, 30 to 40 minutes, depending on the size of the artichoke. Remove the artichokes from the pot and cool.

Mix the bread crumbs and Parmesan cheese in a bowl.

Remove all the leaves from the artichokes, discarding the small center leaves and scooping out the hairy center. Cut the hearts into 6 pieces.

->» «<-

Papaya, Melon, or Mango with Prosciutto

MAKES 20 SERVINGS

½ pound very thinly sliced prosciutto
2 papayas, 1 melon, or 2 mangoes

Cut each thin slice of prosciutto lengthwise into 3 strips.

To use papaya, peel the fruit and cut into approximately 16 wedges. Remove seeds and wrap wedges with strips of prosciutto.

To use a melon for this hors d'oeuvre, cut in half lengthwise and scoop out the seeds with a wooden spoon, taking care not to bruise the flesh of the melon. Cut the melon into quarters, then eighths, and finally sixteenths. Remove the skin from each wedge with a sharp paring knife. Wrap one strip of prosciutto around each melon wedge. The prosciutto should adhere to itself, eliminating the need for toothpicks. (If wedges are too large, cut each into smaller, equal-size pieces.)

To use a mango, cut each fruit lengthwise into 2 pieces, cutting around the elongated center pit.

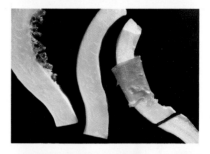

Prosciutto is a cured ham from Italy that should be very thinly sliced for serving. It is excellent wrapped around mango (top), *papaya* (center), *and melon* (bottom).

. . . .

Peel each half and cut into approximately 20 equal-size pieces. Wrap with strips of prosciutto.

VARIATIONS: Wrap halved or quartered ripe figs or blanched asparagus with prosciutto.

In place of prosciutto, wrap fruit with thin slices of Black Forest ham or Westphalian ham.

Wrap bread sticks with strips of prosciutto or ham.

Caramel Brie, a savory-sweet combination that looks like a glistening cake, is the invention of my friend Ruth Leserman.

· ·

Ruth Leserman's Caramel Brie

SERVES 38

1	wheel of Brie (60 percent butterfat), about 2.8 pounds
2	cups granulated sugar
½	cup water
12	to 16 walnut or pecan halves (optional)

Put the Brie on a rack over a large sheet of parchment paper or aluminum foil.

Combine sugar and water in a heavy saucepan and melt the sugar, swirling the pan from time to time. Do not stir. When the mixture begins to boil, cover the pan to allow condensation to drip back down and melt the crystallized sugar on the side of the pan. Uncover the pan after 3 to 5 minutes and continue cooking over high heat until the sugar becomes a deep golden color. The temperature of the caramel should be hard crack, 300°.

Immediately pour the caramel over the cheese to cover the top evenly, allowing the excess to drip down the sides. You may have to tilt the cheese a little to spread the caramel evenly. Be very careful not to touch the hot caramel. Press nuts around the perimeter, if desired. The caramel will harden quickly. Serve within an hour.

Present the cheese with small cheese knives. The guests will have to crack through the caramel coating, but this is part of the fun of eating such an unusual treat.

NOTE: When working with melted sugar or caramel, always keep a bowl of ice water nearby. If you should burn yourself, plunge the burned area into the water.

Brie en Croûte

SERVES 38

1	pound Puff Pastry (page 158)
1	wheel of Brie (60 percent butterfat), about 2.8 pounds
1	egg yolk
4	tablespoons heavy cream

Roll out the puff pastry into a circle appoximately 24 inches in diameter. Place the wheel of Brie in the center and gather up the edges of the dough, as evenly as possible, to encase the cheese completely. You should have a bundle of dough at the top. Tie this with a 12-inch strand of cotton twine to hold it together. Using scissors, trim off excess dough and chill the cheese and dough on a parchment-lined baking sheet for at least 1 hour.

Preheat the oven to 400°.

Combine the egg yolk and the cream and brush the mixture on top of the pastry, covering as much as possible. Bake for 35 to 40 minutes, or until pastry is puffed and golden brown. (You may need to reduce the oven temperature during cooking to keep the pastry from browning too quickly.)

Cool the Brie en croûte on a rack and serve warm or at room temperature.

NOTE: This can be made several hours before serving; it will be fine at room temperature. The cheese can be enclosed in the dough the day before serving, then chilled until it is baked the next day.

· · · · · · · · · · · ·

Right: *Brie en croûte is an impressive dessert cheese made by wrapping a wheel of Brie with puff pastry, which is then gathered on top and tied.*

CHAPTER ELEVEN

The Breakfast Buffet

To some, finger foods for breakfast or brunch might seem a bit peculiar. However, there are many occasions at which the following menu would be very appropriate. A festive get-together after a morning christening, a gathering before or during an exciting sports event, or a breakfast meeting of any sort would warrant the serving of just such an assortment of delicious foods.

The setting of this particular party for fourteen guests was my own country kitchen in our 1805 farmhouse. We covered a large table with an old, worn but still very beautiful quilt. A great terra-cotta saucer filled with forced narcissus bulbs and an oval basket filled with white lilacs, narcissus, and daffo-

. . . .

The breakfast table is brightened with an abundance of white lilacs, narcissus, and daffodils.

dils added color and glorious scent to the room. Because it was still early, and the sun had not yet warmed the kitchen, we lit a fire for warmth as well as ambience.

Drinks were served from pitchers—both the Mary's Knees and the Bloody Marys can be made ahead—and poured into a collection of pressed and cut glass goblets. All the food was displayed in baskets or on old wire cake racks and wooden bread boards, keeping the "country" theme quite evident. A robin's-egg-blue bowl was filled with eggs from our own hens—these were hard-boiled, but cooked or uncooked, such a conglomeration of sizes, shapes, and colors of eggs is sure to attract the attention of one's guests and serve as an interesting centerpiece or table decoration. The hot-from-the-stove New Orleans beignets (a special deep-fried doughnut made from pâte a choux dough), dusted liberally with powdered sugar, were passed as they were made.

The organization of this type of party is quite simple. The crêpes, tartlet shells, and muffins can all be made days in advance and frozen. The fillings for the crêpes, the French toast bread, and the meats for the muffins can be readied the night before. One person must tend the stove during the party to cook the toast and scramble the eggs and fry the beignets, but each of these is quite a simple task requiring little time.

The drinks can be prepared early in the morning. Fresh juices stay fresh for only an hour or two after squeezing, so save this task for last. The Bloody Mary mix can even be made the evening before, but I never add the horseradish or vodka until just before serving.

Because these are finger foods, no plates were provided, but if the party is to be leisurely, it might be nice to add some small plates so that guests could choose a few of the hors d'oeuvres and wander about, away from the buffet table.

For a party of this kind, plan on serving at least two of everything to each guest. If the party is to last longer than one and a half to two hours, enlarge the menu, or make a bit more of everything.

->»«‹-

Menu
for Fourteen

TARTLET SHELLS FILLED WITH SCRAMBLED EGGS

BEIGNETS WITH POWDERED SUGAR

FRENCH TOAST TRIANGLES WITH MAPLE BUTTER

CRÊPES WITH CINNAMON PEARS

CORN MUFFINS WITH SMOKED TURKEY

ORANGE MUFFINS WITH SMOKED DUCK BREAST

ALMOND-STUFFED DATES WITH BACON · ZUCCHINI FRITTERS

MARY'S KNEES · BLOODY MARYS

FRESH ORANGE JUICE AND CHAMPAGNE

TEA · COFFEE

Tartlet Shells Filled with Scrambled Eggs

MAKES 14 TARTLETS

> 2 tablespoons (¼ stick) unsalted butter
> 6 eggs, beaten
> Coarse salt and white pepper to taste
> 14 baked Tartlet Shells (page 150)

In a large heavy skillet over medium heat, melt the butter until it bubbles. Add the eggs all at once and scramble lightly. Do not overcook the eggs. Season with salt and pepper and spoon into the prepared tartlet shells. Serve immediately.

VARIATIONS: Before cooking, add ¼ cup grated Gruyère, ½ cup finely chopped Brie, or 3 tablespoons chopped fresh parsley, chervil, dill, or chives to the eggs.

After spooning scrambled eggs into the tartlet shells, top with 1 teaspoon caviar or a small dollop of Crème Fraîche (page 60).

-->> <<--

Beignets with Powdered Sugar

MAKES ABOUT 40 BEIGNETS

> 2 to 3 cups light vegetable oil
> 1 recipe Pâte à Choux (page 150)
> Powdered sugar

Heat the oil to 365° in a deep skillet. Drop the pâte à choux dough, by tablespoons, into the hot oil and fry on both sides until golden brown, 4 to 6 minutes. Drain on paper towels and serve hot, sprinkled with powdered sugar.

VARIATIONS: Add ¼ cup of chopped jalapeño peppers, ⅓ cup corn kernels, or ⅓ cup grated Cheddar, Gruyère, or Parmesan cheese to the pâte à choux dough before frying. Omit sugar.

-->> <<--

French Toast Triangles with Maple Butter

MAKES 56 PIECES

MAPLE BUTTER
MAKES ¼ CUP

> ¼ cup (½ stick) unsalted butter, softened
> ¼ cup pure Vermont maple syrup
> 14 very thin slices of Pain de Mie (page 158), good store-bought white bread, brioche, or challah
> Light vegetable oil for frying
> 1¼ cups whole milk
> 4 eggs, beaten
> 1 tablespoon sugar
> ½ teaspoon cinnamon
> ¼ cup cognac, bourbon, or Grand Marnier
> Grated rind of 1 orange
> ½ cup sugar mixed with 1 teaspoon cinnamon

To make maple butter, combine butter and syrup in a mixing bowl and blend thoroughly. Refrigerate.

Trim off the bread crusts and cut each slice into four triangles.

Heat the oil to 360° in a large, heavy skillet.

Combine the milk, eggs, sugar, cinnamon, cognac, and orange rind in a shallow dish. Dip the bread slices in the egg mixture and fry on both sides until golden brown, about 2 minutes on each side. Drain on paper towels.

Sprinkle the sugar and cinnamon mixture over the French toast and serve immediately with maple butter.

-->> <<--

Crêpes with Cinnamon Pears

MAKES 28 CRÊPES

> 6 tablespoons (¾ stick) unsalted butter
> 6 pears, peeled, cored, and cut into ¾-inch chunks
> 3 tablespoons sugar
> 1 teaspoon cinnamon
> Grated rind of 1 orange or lemon
> 28 5-inch crêpes (page 155)
> Confectioners' sugar

Melt the butter over medium heat in a large skillet. Add the pears, sugar, cinnamon, and orange or lemon rind and sauté until the pears are just tender, about 8 to 10 minutes.

Let the mixture cool slightly and spoon 1 tablespoon into the center of a crêpe. Fold as if you were making an envelope. Arrange the crêpes on a serving tray and sprinkle with confectioners' sugar.

. . . .

I used old baskets, wire cake racks, and wooden bread boards as serving pieces for this country-style buffet.

Orange Muffins with Smoked Duck Breast

MAKES 28 HORS D'OEUVRES

SMOKED DUCK MARINADE

1	*cup red wine*
2	*pears, peeled, cored, and puréed in a food processor*
2	*bay leaves*
½	*cup currant jelly*
4	*sprigs of thyme*
1	*teaspoon freshly ground black pepper*
1	*teaspoon salt*
2	*duck breasts, bone in (about 2 pounds each)*
28	*small Orange Muffins (page 76)*
½	*cup pear butter or cranberry-orange relish*

Combine all the ingredients for the marinade in a mixing bowl. Pour over the duck breasts and refrigerate for 2 or 3 days, turning the meat once a day. Before smoking, drain the meat and pat it dry.

We smoke the duck breasts over a fire of apple, mesquite, and pear wood for 2 hours in our wooden smokehouse. If using a commercial smoker, smoke the duck breasts according to the manufacturer's instructions.

To serve, cut the meat into thin slices and serve on a sliced orange muffin spread with thick pear butter or cranberry-orange relish.

➤➤≫ ≪≪≪

Corn Muffins with Smoked Turkey

MAKES 36 HORS D'OEUVRES

1½	*cups yellow cornmeal*
1	*cup sifted all-purpose flour*
⅓	*cup sugar*
1	*tablespoon baking powder*
1	*teaspoon salt*
1½	*cups milk*
¾	*cup (1½ sticks) melted butter, cooled*
2	*eggs, slightly beaten*
½	*pound thinly sliced smoked turkey or turkey breasts*

Above left: *We like to make tiny muffins, which we split and fill with meats, flavored mustards, and relishes. Here are orange muffins with turkey and corn muffins with country ham and cranberry relish.* Right: *Light, delectable vegetable fritters.*

. . . .

½	*cup grape jelly or cranberry relish*

Preheat the oven to 400°.

To make the corn muffins, combine cornmeal, flour, sugar, baking powder, and salt in a large bowl. Mix the milk, butter, and eggs together in a medium-size bowl. Stir the milk mixture into the cornmeal mixture just until moistened.

Spoon the batter into buttered tiny muffins pans. Bake until golden, 14 to 16 minutes. Let cool on a wire rack for 5 minutes. Remove from pans and let cool completely.

To serve, put a small amount of smoked turkey on a sliced muffin that has been spread with grape jelly or cranberry relish.

Almond-Stuffed Dates with Bacon

MAKES 60 HORS D'OEUVRES

> 1 pound pitted dates
> 1 4-ounce package blanched whole almonds
> 1¼ pounds very thinly sliced lean bacon

Stuff each date with an almond. Cut bacon strips into thirds and wrap a piece around each date. Secure with a round wooden toothpick.

Put the dates on a foil-lined baking sheet and bake in a preheated 400° oven until the bacon is crisp, about 12 to 15 minutes. Drain on a rack or on paper towels. Serve warm.

NOTE: Prepared dates can be frozen in advance and baked unthawed in a preheated 400° oven until crisp.

VARIATIONS: Small sea scallops, water chestnuts, chicken livers, or oysters and a cilantro leaf can be wrapped with bacon, secured with toothpicks, and broiled until the bacon is crisp, about 6 minutes, turning once. Serve immediately.

Dates can be stuffed with walnuts or pecans.

→»《←

Zucchini Fritters

MAKES 30 2-INCH FRITTERS

BATTER

> 2 tablespoons flour
> 3 eggs, lightly beaten
> Salt and freshly ground black pepper to taste
>
> 2 cups coarsely grated zucchini
> 2 shallots, finely chopped
> 2 tablespoons chopped fresh parsley
> Vegetable oil for frying

GARNISH
> Crème Fraîche (page 60), sour cream, sprouts, herb leaves

In a medium bowl, mix the batter ingredients until smooth. Add the grated zucchini, shallots, and parsley, and combine thoroughly.

Heat a small amount of vegetable oil (⅛ inch deep) in a heavy skillet. Drop the fritter batter in the hot oil by tablespoons, frying until golden on each side, about 4 to 6 minutes. Drain on paper towels.

Garnish the fritters as desired and serve hot.

VARIATIONS: An equal amount of other grated vegetables and spices can be substituted for the zucchini, shallots, and parlsey. Try grated carrots, 2 teaspoons grated ginger, and ½ teaspoon chopped fresh tarragon; grated parsnip, 2 very finely chopped scallions, and ½ teaspoon freshly grated nutmeg; or grated white turnip, 1 small chopped onion, 1 grated carrot, and cinnamon to taste. You can also use a combination of some or all of the above, with or without spices and seasonings.

→»《←

Mary's Knees

MAKES 4 DRINKS

> 1 cup freshly squeezed orange juice
> ⅓ cup freshly squeezed lemon juice
> ⅓ cup freshly squeezed lime juice
> ½ cup vodka, or to taste
> ⅓ cup Grand Marnier

Combine all the ingredients in a large pitcher and pour over ice in stemmed goblets.

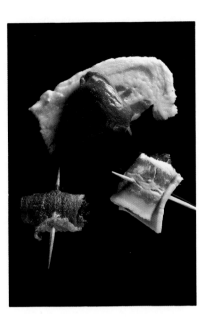

Almond-stuffed dates wrapped with bacon are a favorite hors d'oeuvre, adaptable for many occasions. The sweetness of the date, the crunchiness of the nut, and the crispness of the bacon combine to make a perfect finger food.

. . . .

Bloody Marys

MAKES 2 DRINKS

> 1 cup good tomato juice
> ⅓ cup vodka, or to taste
> 2 teaspoons prepared horseradish
> Tabasco sauce to taste
> Freshly ground black pepper to taste
> Juice of 1 lime

GARNISH
> Cucumber spears or celery sticks

Combine the tomato juice, vodka, horseradish, Tabasco sauce, black pepper, and lime juice in a pitcher. Adjust seasoning to taste and serve on the rocks in large bubble glasses. Garnish with spears of cucumber or celery.

CHAPTER TWELVE

Tex-Mex Hors d'Oeuvres

With America's renewed interest in the cuisines of all its regions and territories, one cannot overlook a pseudo-Mexican type of cooking that has become known as Tex-Mex. It is a combination of Mexican cooking found in Texas and in other parts of the Southwest. It often incorporates dishes that are found in California, and in the kitchens of Salvadorans living in California, and in New York kitchens where the cooks think about Mexico but never visit. It is a simple, wonderful, robust kind of cooking that lends itself beautifully to finger-food-type menus, served with pitchers of margaritas, goblets of tequila and tonic, and icy mugs of Mexican beer.

This party for twenty-four was a great success. There is something delightfully informal about this type of menu, and the colorful (and inexpensive) decorations can create an atmosphere of great conviviality. You might even stipulate Mexican dress on the invitation and be extraordinarily pleased at what shows up. If you have any help, request that they, too, dress appropriately. The crew for this party was attired in cotton whites, sashed around the waist with colorful Mexican scarves. Cover tables, bars, and buffets with hot colors—cloths can be rented in bright pinks, yellows, and oranges. Drape Mexican serapes over the tables. Skulls of cattle, lassos, sombreros, Mexican clay pots and dishes, potted cacti, and strings and strings of colorful hot peppers are great decorations.

It is interesting to note that almost everything on the menu can be purchased throughout America. Most freezer sections of large groceries have tortillas, avocados

. . . .

Salt-rimmed glasses of refreshing margaritas are a perfect accompaniment to south-of-the-border foods. Fresh lime juice is indispensable in making the best margarita.

are generally available, and great varieties of chili peppers are appearing in supermarkets. Mail-order catalogs offer some of the ingredients for those who have difficulty locating items locally.

We made about two of each hors d'oeuvre per person. Of course, nachos and tortilla chips and quesadilla wedges must be made in great quantities and offered liberally. Have lots of beer (Mexican, of course) in tubs full of ice, and for twenty-four guests at least two or three quarts of freshly squeezed lime juice for margaritas. I prefer Cointreau or Grand Marnier to Triple Sec for margaritas, and I now use the best white tequila rather than gold tequila for these drinks. I use gold tequila for tonic drinks and to mix with freshly squeezed orange juice. A small table set with salt-rimmed goblets, pitchers of lime juice, and an electric blender will facilitate the making of the drinks.

Much of the menu can be prepared in advance. The empanaditas can be made way ahead and frozen, uncooked. The seviche should be made six to eight hours in advance and the chips fried the morning of the party. If the guacamole is made more than five minutes before the party, cover the bowl with plastic wrap, making sure the wrap touches the surface of the mixture so no air can turn it brown. Guacamole is best made right before eating; to make the task easier, combine all the ingredients except the avocado in a bowl ahead of time and add the avocado last.

A Tex-Mex party can be held indoors or out. I like the option of using a poolside or terrace for part of the party and the indoors for a buffet. On a warm, beautiful day I would stage the entire party outdoors.

Menu
for Twenty-four

TORTILLA CHIPS
TOMATILLO SAUCE, GUACAMOLE, SALSA ROJA,
NACHOS · PICO DE GALLO SAUCE
TACOS LA SALSA · QUESADILLAS
CORN CUPS FILLED WITH BEEF CHILI
SEVICHE OF SCALLOPS · BEAN BURRITOS
TORTAS DE COLIFLOR · GORDITAS
FRESH CRAB EMPANADITAS · SHRIMP AND PEPPER TORTILLAS
MARGARITAS · TEQUILA AND TONIC · MEXICAN BEER

We always make our own tortilla chips—and lots of them—to serve with freshly made spicy red and green salsas, and guacamole.

· ·

Tortilla Chips

Tortilla chips (tostados) for nachos (page 130) and for snacks to dip in salsa can be made very easily. Cut fresh corn tortillas into sixths and lightly fry the wedges in hot (375°) vegetable or corn oil. Drain chips well on paper towels or on a rack. Shake hot tostados in a paper bag with table salt and one crushed garlic clove. Serve warm or at room temperature.

→≫≪←

Tomatillo Sauce

MAKES 1½ CUPS

1   *pound fresh tomatillos, or 1 10-ounce can of tomatillos, well drained*
2   *fresh jalapeño peppers, seeded and chopped (use canned if necessary)*
1   *cup fresh cilantro leaves*
1   *garlic clove, peeled and chopped*
1   *white onion, peeled and chopped*

Salt and freshly ground black pepper to taste

If you are using fresh tomatillos, peel the paperlike skin away and boil for 10 minutes in salted water. Drain all but ½ cup of the liquid (cooking or canning liquid), and purée the tomatillos in a food processor with the reserved liquid and the remaining ingredients.

Serve as a green salsa with tortilla chips.

NOTE: Tomatillos are green Spanish tomatoes and are often available fresh in Spanish or Mexican groceries.

→≫≪←

Guacamole

MAKES 1½ QUARTS

3   *ripe tomatoes, seeded and coarsely chopped*
¼   *cup chopped fresh cilantro leaves*
1   *medium white onion, minced*
2   *garlic cloves, minced*

¼   *to ½ cup lime juice to taste*
    Minced and seeded fresh chili peppers (such as jalapeños) to taste
8   *very ripe but unbruised avocados*
    Salt to taste

Mix the tomatoes, cilantro, onion, garlic, lime juice, chili peppers, and salt in a glass or pottery mixing bowl.

Immediately before serving, peel and coarsely mash the avocados. Stir in the tomato mixture. Season with salt and serve at once.

NOTE: If the guacamole is made in advance, add one or two avocado pits to the mixture, and cover the surface of the guacamole with plastic wrap to keep the air from darkening it.

→≫≪←

Salsa Roja

MAKES 1 QUART

This sauce is best when made at least 6 hours before serving. It can be mild with no peppers or as hot as you like. The salsa can also be used as a base for quick guacamole—just add some avocados to it.

8   *ripe tomatoes, seeded and chopped*
½   *cup loosely packed cilantro leaves*
2   *medium white onions, minced*
2   *garlic cloves, minced*
½   *cup chopped fresh Italian flat leaf parsley*
½   *cup light olive oil*
    Salt and freshly ground black pepper to taste
3   *fresh jalapeño peppers, seeded and minced, or 3 canned jalapeño peppers, minced (optional)*

Combine all the ingredients in a mixing bowl. Season to taste and refrigerate until ready to use.

Nachos are so good you can never make enough. These are mounded with black beans, cheese, and peppers, but the variations are limitless.

· ·

Nachos

Nachos are very popular appetizers that disappear as quickly as they are made. Nachos are chips that are arranged in an ovenproof dish, topped with an assortment of cheeses, beans, peppers, and onions, and heated in a hot oven until the cheese melts. They can also be heated under a hot broiler. Top nachos with your choice of:

Spoonfuls of refried red beans, coarsely chopped red onion, and grated Monterey Jack cheese; heat until cheese melts.

Black beans, chopped jalapeño peppers, and grated cheese melted in the oven, then topped with dollops of sour cream and guacamole.

Shreds of hot and sweet peppers, grated cheese, and chopped red onion melted in the oven, served hot.

Spoonfuls of chili and grated cheese melted in the oven, then topped with dollops of sour cream.

Thin slices of chorizo (Mexican sausage), finely chopped scallions or green onions, grated Monterey Jack, sharp Cheddar, or jalapeño cheese melted in the oven and served hot.

⇢≫⟨⟨←

Pico de Gallo Sauce

MAKES 2 TO 3 CUPS

This sauce is best when made less than 2 or 3 hours before serving. It is delicious with tortilla chips, and it is a wonderful topping for Tacos la Salsa (recipe follows).

> 4 **large, very ripe, red tomatoes, chopped**

> ½ **cup finely chopped scallions**
> 3 **jalapeño peppers, seeded and finely chopped**
> 2 **garlic cloves, peeled and finely minced**
> ¼ **cup freshly squeezed lime juice**
> ½ **cup finely chopped cilantro**
> 1 **teaspoon finely chopped fresh oregano**
> **Salt and freshly ground black pepper to taste**

Combine all ingredients and cover and refrigerate until serving time.

⇢≫⟨⟨←

Tacos la Salsa

MAKES ABOUT 20

These tacos have the most flavor when the meats are grilled over charcoal. Making them in large numbers simplifies the process.

> 2 **pounds boneless chicken breasts, skinned**
> 2 **pounds flank steak, well trimmed of all fat**
> 36 **scallions**
> 1 **package (about 20) corn tortillas**
> ¼ **cup olive oil**

To prepare the chicken for grilling, cut the breast into flat, thin pieces. Grill over hot coals for a minute or two on each side, just enough to cook it and blacken it slightly. Slice into strips.

Grill whole flank steak over hot coals for approximately 4 minutes on each side (I prefer it slightly rare). With a very sharp knife, slice the steak crosswise into thin strips.

Clean and peel the scallions, leaving the root end intact. Grill over hot coals. Use as a garnish for both the chicken and flank steak.

Lightly brush each tortilla with ol-

Wedges of cheese-filled
quesadillas and grilled beef and
chicken tacos la salsa should be
served hot. Small pattypan squashes
hold garnishes of chopped
onions and sour cream.

. . . .

ive oil and place on the grill for a
few seconds, just to heat one side.
Top the tortilla with either grilled
chicken or flank steak and scallions. Serve tacos with a variety of
salsas, sour cream, grated cheese,
and shredded lettuce.

Quesadillas

MAKES 8 PORTIONS

Quesadillas are two flour tortillas filled
with cheese and chilies and fried. Serve
with salsa and, if you wish, guacamole
and sour cream.

Oil for frying
½ **cup grated cheese**
   (Monterey Jack or
   Cheddar)
1 **to 3 cherry tomatoes, sliced**
1 **small serrano or jalapeño**
   chili, roasted and chopped

2 **large flour tortillas**
   Salt to taste

Heat ¼ inch of oil in a frying pan.

Sprinkle the cheese, tomatoes, and
chili on top of one tortilla. Cover
with the other and fry the quesadilla in hot oil for 2 minutes,
weighting it down if necessary with
a small frying pan. Turn the quesadilla and fry for 2 more minutes.

Drain on paper towel, season to
taste, and cut into eighths. Serve
immediately.

Corn Cups Filled with Beef Chili

MAKES 2½ DOZEN
HORS D'OEUVRES

BEEF CHILI
MAKES 1 QUART

3 slices of bacon
1 pound beef, thinly sliced and slivered
1 onion, finely chopped
2 garlic cloves, minced
1 jalapeño pepper, thinly sliced
1 teaspoon cumin
2 tablespoons chili powder
1 1½-pound can of whole tomatoes
Cornmeal (optional)

CORN CUP DOUGH

6 tablespoons (¾ stick) unsalted butter, at room temperature
3 ounces cream cheese, at room temperature
1 cup all-purpose flour
½ cup cornmeal
Pinch of salt

To make the chili, heat a pan over a medium-high flame and sauté the bacon for a few minutes, until some of the fat is rendered. Add the beef slivers and onion to the pan, reduce the heat to medium low, and sauté for 5 minutes. Add the garlic, pepper, cumin, and chili powder. Cook until the jalapeño pepper is soft, about 15 minutes.

Add the tomatoes, stir well, and cook over low heat until the liquid has evaporated, about 1 hour. If necessary, add 1 to 2 tablespoons cornmeal to thicken the mixture. No liquid should be left in the pan before filling the corn cups.

Preheat the oven to 350°.

To make the corn cups, cream together the butter and cream cheese with a wooden spoon or electric mixer.

Combine the flour, cornmeal, and salt. Add it, a little at a time, to the butter mixture, stirring constantly until well incorporated. Knead it lightly with your hands.

Divide the dough into 1-inch balls and press them into small muffin tins, using your thumbs to form cups inside the mold. The dough cups should be as even as possible and come up to the top of the tins.

Bake for 20 minutes, or until golden brown. Fill with hot beef chili and serve.

VARIATIONS: Two tablespoons of a variety of minced ingredients can be added to the corn cup dough. Try jalapeño peppers, scallions, chives, green onions, or red peppers.

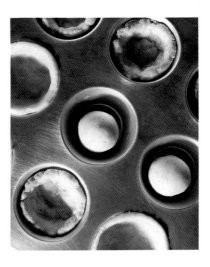

1 green tomato (optional)
½ cup white wine
2 garlic cloves, minced
1 teaspoon cumin
  Salt and freshly ground
  black pepper to taste
2 tablespoons (¼ stick)
  unsalted butter
1 whole jalapeño pepper,
  thinly sliced
½ cup parsley, chopped
8 sprigs cilantro, chopped

Slice the chicken breast into pieces small enough to fit into the corn cups. Sauté in olive oil, for 3 to 4 minutes. Set aside.

Purée the olives, Italian peppers, and green tomato in a blender until smooth. Add to the chicken, along with the wine, garlic, cumin, and salt and pepper, and cook over medium-low heat for about 20 to 30 minutes.

Heat the butter in a pan and sauté the jalapeño pepper, parsley, and cilantro over medium heat for 2 minutes. Add to the chili. Serve chili warm in corn cups.

CHILI PEPPERS AND CHEESE

MAKES 1½ CUPS

2 jalapeño peppers
  (fresh or canned), seeded
  and chopped
1 fresh chili pepper, seeded
  and finely chopped
1 sweet red pepper, seeded
  and finely chopped
3 tablespoons olive oil
1 cup grated sharp
  Cheddar or Monterey
  Jack cheese
  Salt and freshly ground
  black pepper to taste

Sauté the peppers in olive oil until soft, 5 to 6 minutes. Mix with the grated cheese, season, and spoon into corn cups immediately.

Left: *Old Mexican pottery plates offer an authentic background for these ever-popular corn cups filled with beef chili, green chili, and guacamole.* Above: *To make a corn cup, butter tiny muffin tins, roll the corn mixture into 1-inch balls, and press into cups with your thumbs. This makes a perfect, bite-size hors d'oeuvre.*

. . . .

CHORIZO AND SCRAMBLED EGGS

MAKES APPROXIMATELY 1 CUP

3 tablespoons unsalted
  butter or olive oil
6 eggs, beaten
½ cup chopped chorizo
2 tablespoons chopped
  scallions
  Salt and freshly ground
  pepper to taste

Melt the butter in a heavy frying pan. Scramble the eggs with the chorizo (a peppery pork sausage) in the pan, adding the scallions at the very end. Season with salt and pepper and serve in corn cups.

Other Variations

Corn Salad (page 32)
Guacamole (page 129)
Spicy Black Beans (page 134)

Filling Variations
GREEN CHILI

MAKES 1 QUART

1 pound chicken breast,
  boned and skinned
3 tablespoons olive oil
20 green olives, pitted
6 green Italian frying
  peppers, seeded and
  chopped

TEX-MEX HORS D'OEUVRES

Seviche of Scallops

MAKES 30 TO 40 HORS D'OEUVRES

- 1   pound fresh bay scallops
- 3/4 cup fresh lime juice
- 4   scallions, minced
- 1   fresh chili pepper, minced
- 1   teaspoon freshly ground black pepper
- 2   tablespoons chopped cilantro
- 1/4 cup olive oil

GARNISH
   Lettuce leaves (optional)

Combine the scallops, lime juice, scallions, chili pepper, black pepper, cilantro, and olive oil in a glass or stainless steel mixing bowl. Let stand for 2 to 4 hours in the refrigerator, stirring occasionally, or refrigerate overnight.

To serve, skewer scallops on toothpicks or arrange on lettuce leaves.

VARIATION: Substitute 1 pound fresh tuna, salmon, or sole cut into 1/4-inch cubes for the scallops.

Bean Burritos

MAKES 12 TO 15 SMALL BURRITOS

- 1   15-ounce can of pinto or red kidney beans
- 1/2 cup minced red onion
- 2   tablespoons chopped cilantro
- 1   tablespoon freshly ground black pepper
- 1   tablespoon fresh oregano
- 1   package small flour tortillas (about 15)

Preheat the oven to 325°.

Drain the beans, reserving one-fourth of the liquid.

Combine the beans and reserved liquid, onion, cilantro, pepper, and oregano in a mixing bowl.

Spread 1½ tablespoons of the bean mixture on one half of the tortilla. Roll once, tuck both ends toward the center, and continue rolling. Arrange the burritos in an oven-proof dish and cover with foil.

Bake the burritos for 10 minutes, or until they are thoroughly warm. Serve immediately.

Filling Variation
SPICY BLACK BEANS
MAKES 1 CUP

- 1   cup dried black beans, washed and soaked in cold water overnight
- 1   large white onion, peeled and finely chopped
- 1   garlic clove, peeled and finely chopped
- 4   tablespoons lard
- 1   or 2 jalapeño peppers, seeded and finely chopped
- 1/4 cup cilantro leaves, finely chopped
     Salt and freshly ground black pepper to taste

Drain the black beans and put in a saucepan with water to cover. Bring to a boil and cook until beans are soft. This may take an hour or longer; add more water to keep

. . . .

Below left: **Seviche is very simple to make, since there is no real cooking involved.** *Below right:* **Fried cauliflower balls, bean burritos, and seviche (here served in lettuce cups) are surrounded by fresh tomatillos.**

beans covered while cooking if necessary. As the beans begin to soften, let the water evaporate.

When beans are done, sauté the onion and garlic in lard until soft but not browned. Add the cooked beans and any liquid, and cook 30 minutes more over low heat. Add the chopped jalapeños and cilantro and season to taste.

–>>)(<<–

Tortas de Coliflor

MAKES 30 CAULIFLOWER BALLS

1	*medium head of cauliflower, steamed until tender*
1½	*cups grated white Cheddar cheese*
½	*teaspoon salt*
¼	*teaspoon freshly ground black pepper Pinch of cayenne pepper*
¼	*teaspoon grated nutmeg*
4	*tablespoons flour*
1	*tablespoon chopped fresh parsley (optional)*
4	*egg whites, beaten to soft peaks Vegetable oil for frying*
1½	*cups bread crumbs (preferably Japanese)*

Put the cooked cauliflower in the bowl of a food processor with the cheese, salt, black pepper, cayenne pepper, nutmeg, and parsley, if desired. Process until coarsely chopped.

Put the cauliflower mixture in a bowl, add the flour, and stir until smooth. Add the parsley, if desired, and combine well. Fold the softly beaten egg whites into the mixture.

In a heavy wok or cast iron skillet, heat 3 inches of oil to 360°.

Drop tablespoonfuls of the cauliflower mixture into the bread crumbs and coat well. Roll into balls and fry in the oil until golden brown, 4 to 6 minutes. Drain on paper towels and serve hot.

NOTE: Japanese bread crumbs are available in Oriental markets.

–>>)(<<–

Gorditas

MAKES 24

Gorditas are half pockets of thick corn tortillas, very similar in appearance to pita bread, that are filled with spicy scrambled eggs and chorizo.

12	*4-inch corn tortillas*
8	*eggs, beaten*
¼	*cup olive oil*
1	*cup coarsely chopped chorizo*
3	*canned jalapeño peppers, coarsely chopped Freshly ground black pepper to taste*

Cut tortillas in half, wrap in foil, and warm in a 325° oven for approximately 10 minutes. The tortillas should open up like pockets.

While the tortillas are warming, scramble eggs in olive oil in a heavy pan, and heat the chorizo in a small amount of olive oil in another. When the eggs are done, combine with the remaining ingredients in a bowl.

Fill half tortillas with warm egg–sausage mixture and serve. For guests with hotter palates, serve hot sauce and a small carafe of white vinegar alongside the gorditas.

. . . .

Gorditas garnished with fresh cilantro are served from a Mexican pottery bowl. Salsa verde and other garnishes surround them.

Fresh Crab Empanaditas

MAKES 30 EMPANADITAS

PASTRY

- 2½ cups sifted all-purpose flour
- ¼ pound (1 stick) unsalted butter or lard
- 1 teaspoon sugar
- 1 teaspoon salt
- 1 egg
- ½ cup ice water

FILLING

- 1 tablespoon unsalted butter
- 1 medium onion, finely chopped
- 1 ripe tomato, seeded and finely chopped
- ¾ pound fresh lump crabmeat or frozen snow crab
- 1 tablespoon chopped fresh parsley
- ¼ cup tiny capers
- 1 tablespoon rice wine vinegar
- ½ teaspoon fresh thyme
  Salt and freshly ground black pepper to taste

EGG GLAZE

- 1 egg lightly beaten with 1 tablespoon water

Make the pastry in a food processor or by hand, following the method for tart shells on page 150. Chill until ready to use.

To make the filling, heat the butter in a large skillet and sauté the onion and tomato over medium-high heat for 6 to 8 minutes, or until soft. Add the remaining ingredients. Cook for 5 minutes, stirring often. Remove the pan from the heat and let cool.

On a lightly floured board, roll out the dough to ⅛ inch thick. Cut the dough into 2½-inch rounds, using a biscuit cutter or a glass.

Tiny crab "empanaditas" are a perfect finger food.

. . . .

Put 1 teaspoon of the filling in the center of the pastry rounds. Wet the edges with cold water and fold the pastry in half. Seal the edges by pressing firmly all around with the tines of a fork.

Put the empanaditas on a buttered baking sheet and refrigerate until ready to bake.

Preheat the oven to 375°.

Brush the tops of the empanaditas with the egg glaze. Bake for 25 minutes, or until golden. Serve hot.

NOTE: The empanaditas can be made in advance, frozen (unbaked), and baked in a 375° oven for 30 to 35 minutes.

Filling Variations

Beef Chili (page 132)
Green Chili (page 133)
Chili Peppers and Cheese (page 133)
Spicy Black Beans (page 134)
Shredded pork
Chorizo sausage
Raisins and rice

Shrimp and Pepper Tortillas

MAKES 12 to 16 HORS D'OEUVRES

- 12 large shrimps
- ½ cup olive oil
- 1 red bell pepper, julienned
- 1 yellow bell pepper, julienned
- 1 Italian frying pepper, julienned
- 1 banana pepper (a long, pale yellow pepper, also called a Cubanelle), julienned
- 3 garlic cloves, minced
- 4 to 5 assorted small chili peppers (jalapeño, cayenne, serrano, etc.)
- 4 corn tortillas, cut into quarters, or 12 small, 6-inch tortillas

Clean, shell, and devein the shrimps, leaving tails intact.

Heat the oil over medium heat and sauté the julienned peppers and garlic for 2 minutes. Add the shrimps and whole chili peppers and cook for about 3 minutes, until shrimps are cooked thoroughly and have turned a bright orange. Do not overcook. Spoon the mixture onto tortillas that have been steamed, fried, or slightly blackened over a flame.

→>> «<<

Margaritas

MAKES 4 LARGE DRINKS

- Cut limes
- Coarse salt
- Ice cubes
- 1¼ cups freshly squeezed lime juice
- 1 cup best-quality white tequila
- ⅓ cup Cointreau
- ⅓ cup sugar (or more to taste)

To salt-rim the glasses, rub a cut lime around the rim of stemmed goblets (I like to serve margaritas in bubble goblets). Fill a saucer with salt and dip the goblet, upside down, into the salt. Refrigerate goblets until ready to use.

Fill a blender jar three-quarters full of ice cubes. Pour the lime juice, te-quila, and Cointreau over the ice. Add the sugar and blend, starting slowly and then setting the blender at high speed, until the ice is very finely chopped and the mixture is frothy. Taste for sweetness, adding more sugar if necessary. Blend a few seconds more and pour into the salt-rimmed glasses. Serve immediately.

A single large shrimp, quickly sautéed in oil with a colorful variety of peppers—both hot and sweet—makes an unbelievably good and special hors d'oeuvre when served on a small, blackened corn tortilla. If small 6-inch tortillas are not available, you can substitute larger ones cut into quarters.

TEX-MEX HORS D'OEUVRES

CHAPTER THIRTEEN

Fancy Cocktails

W e had this party at our home not long ago. I love to have twenty or thirty people in for drinks and finger food before a dinner party, antique-show benefit, or evening community event that will include lots of activity and late-night supping. Twenty guests is actually a perfect number for our home, and this party worked wonderfully.

I asked one person to help me in the kitchen, because I needed to leave with the rest of the party right after cocktails to attend a theater benefit. Normally a menu of this simplicity can be accomplished by one person. It would be necessary to have another tend bar (one's husband, for example), or to have a self-service bar set up somewhere. However, since this party was "fancy," I wanted to have the drinks offered to the guests.

For this party I used colored glass for the

drinks and copper trays, which are a very nice change from silver trays or baskets and make food look beautiful. We set most of the food on the sideboard and dining-room table, and I passed the very few hot items—the chicken on skewers and the tortellini. We had second trays of everything prepared in the kitchen, so that trays were merely replaced, not taken away to be refilled, leaving an empty space on the sideboard. This is a very good method of serving, the only requirement being a plethora of trays or platters. But if cocktails are a usual way to entertain, then a small collection of trays should not be a problem.

The party lasted for an hour and a half. I prepared two or three of each hors d'oeuvre for each person. Prepared in advance were the sausage rolls (frozen, and baked right before serving), marinated shrimps, crabmeat filling, beets for the endive, mushroom-parsley filling for the radicchio, and chicken for the skewers. On the day of the party, snow peas were blanched and some split, some separated, yellow peppers were cut up and skewered with the chicken, tortellini was cooked and tossed with oil (it was reheated just before serving, in a steamer), and baby red potatoes were steamed and kept hot in a small cooler. (Potatoes will stay hot for up to six hours in a well-insulated cooler, but since the interior of the cooler will buckle somewhat with use, it's a good idea to save it just for this purpose.)

The last-minute assembling of all the hors d'oeuvres and the arranging of trays was very easily accomplished by my kitchen helper. Before the party, I went over a list I had prepared of the various things that had to be done, and during the party I had to do just a little rearranging to make each tray perfect. It is very important that whoever is helping know exactly how things are to look—hors d'oeuvres should be precise, and it is a good idea to make a sample of each to use as a model for the evening.

We had an open bar—that is, we served whatever anyone requested, from martinis, Manhattans, and Bloody Marys to white wine spritzers. Andy made the drinks, a job he actually found quite challenging and fun.

→≫≪←

Menu
for Twenty

SKEWERED TORTELLINI · CHICKEN SKEWERS
RED POTATOES WITH SOUR CREAM AND CAVIAR
SHRIMP WRAPPED IN SNOW PEAS
SNOW PEAS WITH CRABMEAT FILLING
ENDIVE WITH BEETS AND MUSTARD SPROUTS
SAUSAGE ROLL PUFFS · FILLET OF BEEF
SMOKED TROUT WITH HORSERADISH CREAM
RADICCHIO WITH WILD MUSHROOMS AND PARSLEY
OPEN BAR

Mache leaves and enoki mushrooms garnish an Irish treamer that holds two types of skewered hors d'oeuvres: egg and spinach tortellini, and bite-size chunks of chicken and peppers.

. . . .

Skewered Tortellini

MAKES APPROXIMATELY
40 SKEWERS

PARMESAN LEMON DIP
MAKES 1 ¼ CUPS, ENOUGH FOR
40 SKEWERS

   1   *cup Crème Fraîche*
        (page 60)
   ¼   *cup grated Parmesan*
        cheese
        Juice of 2 lemons
        Grated zest of 2 lemons
   3   *cloves Roasted Garlic*
        (page 29), peeled and
        crushed
   1½ *pounds tortellini*
        Olive oil

Combine all the ingredients for the dip in a small mixing bowl. Set aside until ready to use.

Bring a large kettle of lightly salted water to a boil and cook the tortellini until just tender. Drain the pasta and sprinkle with some olive oil to prevent sticking.

Put 2 warm tortellini on small, 6-inch skewers and serve immediately with the dip.

⇒⟫⟪⇐

Chicken Skewers

MAKES 40 SKEWERS

   1½ *pounds boneless, skinless*
        chicken breast
   1   *tablespoon balsamic*
        vinegar or red wine
        vinegar
   ⅓   *cup white or red wine*
   ½   *cup chopped chutney*
   ¼   *cup olive oil*
   3   *peppers, green and*
        yellow, seeded and cut
        into ½-inch squares
        or strips

Cut the chicken into ¾-inch cubes. Put in a large mixing bowl. Add the vinegar, wine, chutney, and olive oil and stir to combine. Marinate for at least 4 hours, or overnight.

Drain the chicken and put on skewers 6 inches long, alternating 2 pieces of chicken with pieces of yellow or green peppers.

Broil or grill over hot coals for 8 to 10 minutes. Serve hot.

VARIATIONS: Chicken can also be skewered with apple chunks, scallions, pineapple chunks, whole mushrooms, or pieces of celery.

Red Potatoes with Sour Cream and Caviar

Choose the smallest, most blemish-free red-skinned potatoes. Allow 2 or 3 potatoes per person. They should be washed, and either boiled gently until tender or baked in a 350° oven until tender, about 30 minutes.

To serve, cut the potatoes in half and place cut side down on trays. With a melon-ball scoop, spoon out some of the top to create a small cavity.

Fill with a dollop of sour cream and top with red caviar (salmon), black caviar (Sevruga or Osetra), or golden caviar (whitefish).

Topping Variations

Sautéed onion
Crumbled crisp bacon
Sour cream and fresh herbs
Chopped ham
Chopped scallions
Grated cheese
Chopped walnuts
Alfalfa sprouts
Coarse salt, freshly ground black pepper, and melted butter

→»«←

Shrimp Wrapped in Snow Peas

MAKES ABOUT
30 HORS D'OEUVRES

1   bay leaf
1   pound medium shrimps (30 to 32), peeled and deveined

SHRIMP MARINADE

1   tablespoon champagne vinegar
1   tablespoon sweet rice wine vinegar
1/3   cup olive oil
1   large garlic clove, crushed
15   to 20 snow peas

Add the bay leaf to a large pot of water and bring to a rapid boil. Add the shrimps and cook until just done (2 to 3 minutes). Be sure not to overcook. Drain the shrimps, immerse in very cold water to cool, and drain again. Put them in a glass or stainless steel bowl.

Mix the marinade ingredients in a bowl or a covered jar. Shake or mix well and pour over the shrimps. Stir to coat well, cover the bowl, and re-frigerate for 1 to 2 days, tossing every 12 hours.

String the snow peas and blanch in boiling water for 30 seconds. Chill in ice water and drain. Split the pods lengthwise, so that you have 30 to 40 separate halves.

Wrap a pea pod around each shrimp, and fasten by piercing with a round natural-wood toothpick. Serve cold or at room temperature.

NOTE: Wrapped shrimps can be stuck into a large head of cabbage. Cut off a bit of the bottom of the cabbage so it stands upright.

Left: Red bliss potatoes, roasted until tender, are served with a topping of salmon caviar and sour cream. A calendula posy and one of my copper heart trays make this an especially elegant presentation. Right: *The snow pea is a versatile food, used here as a container for a crab and red pepper salad and to wrap around marinated shrimp. The copper tray is garnished with galax leaves and bachelor buttons.* Center: *After a 30-second blanching, snow peas can be left whole for crudités, split for filling, or halved for wrapping.* Bottom: *Herb cheese and salmon mousse can be decoratively piped into split peas; crab salad must be inserted with a spatula.*

. . . .

1   *red pepper, julienned into 1-inch strips*
     Juice of ½ lemon
     Salt and freshly ground pepper to taste

Blanch the snow peas in lightly salted boiling water for 30 seconds. Cool in ice water and drain well.

Combine all the ingredients for the crabmeat filling in a mixing bowl.

With the sharp point of a paring knife, split the snow peas on the curved side. Stuff some of the crabmeat filling in each split snow pea. Arrange on a serving platter.

Filling Variations

HERB CHEESE

MAKES 50 HORS D'OEUVRES

8   *ounces cream cheese, at room temperature*
¼   *cup chopped fresh parsley or chervil*
¼   *cup chopped fresh dill*
1   *garlic clove, minced*
     Black pepper to taste

GARNISH
     Sprouts or watercress

Snow Peas with Crabmeat Filling

MAKES 50 TO 60 HORS D'OEUVRES

50 to 60 tender young snow peas

CRABMEAT FILLING

MAKES ABOUT 1½ CUPS

1   *8-ounce package of cream cheese, at room temperature*
1   *4-ounce package of frozen snow crabmeat, thawed and drained*

Blend the cream cheese, parsley, dill, garlic, and pepper in a mixing bowl until smooth. Spread about ¾ teaspoon of the mixture on the bottom of each endive leaf, using a small spoon, spatula, or pastry bag with tip. Garnish as desired.

Other Variations

Smoked Salmon Mousse (page 72)
Bleu de Bresse (page 72)
St. André or Boursin cheese, at room temperature

Endive with Beets and Mustard Sprouts

MAKES ABOUT
50 HORS D'OEUVRES

> 6 to 8 small beets
> Zest of 2 oranges
> 2 tablespoons cider vinegar
> 4 tablespoons walnut oil
> 4 to 5 heads of endive

GARNISH
> **Mustard sprouts**

Cook the beets in boiling water until tender, 15 to 20 minutes, depending on size of beets; drain and let cool. When the beets have cooled, peel them and cut into thin julienne strips. Cut the orange zest into julienne strips. Marinate the beets in the vinegar, oil, and orange zest overnight.

To serve, separate the leaves of the endives by cutting off a small portion of the bottom of each endive and loosening the leaves. Don't tear off the leaves, because the edges will become ragged.

Spoon a small amount of beets and orange zest onto the endive leaves and garnish with mustard sprouts. Arrange endive on a tray and serve.

VEGETABLE PURÉE

MAKES 50 HORS D'OEUVRES

> 1 pound cooked vegetables (parsnips, carrots, turnips, sweet potato, butternut squash, or celery root)
> 2 tablespoons (¼ stick) unsalted butter, at room temperature
> 8 ounces cream cheese, at room temperature
> Salt and freshly ground black pepper to taste

GARNISH
> **Watercress, rugola, strips of radicchio, sprouts, or mache leaves**

Mash the well-drained cooked vegetables and combine with the butter and cream cheese until smooth. Season to taste and spoon or pipe onto individual endive leaves.

VARIATIONS: Enrich the flavors of the puréed vegetables by adding 1 ripe, chopped pear to parsnips or sweet potatoes; 1 roasted red pepper to parsnips; 1 chopped apple to the butternut squash; or ½ cup cooked rutabaga to the carrots. Purée the mixture and season with ground nutmeg, coriander, or cinnamon.

GORGONZOLA-STILTON CHEESE

MAKES 50 HORS D'OEUVRES

> ½ pound Gorgonzola-Stilton cheese
> 8 ounces cream cheese, at room temperature

GARNISH
> **Sprouts, watercress, or mache leaves**

Soften half the Gorgonzola-Stilton cheese to room temperature; cut the rest into small, thin pieces.

With a wooden spoon or in the bowl of an electric mixer, cream the softened cheeses until smooth. No more than an hour before serving, put this mixture in a pastry bag and pipe it onto individual endive spears with a flat or zigzag tip. Put a small piece of cut Gorgonzola-Stilton on top, and garnish as desired. If endive is not to be served within 15 minutes, cover the spears with plastic wrap and refrigerate.

Other Variations
> **Smoked Salmon Mousse (page 72)**
> **Smoked Trout Mousse (page 73)**
> **Herb Cheese (page 143)**

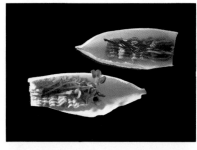

. . . .

Individual leaves of endive are excellent bases for fillings. Clockwise from upper left: *slices of pear and apple and watercress leaves garnish piped vegetable purées; slivers of red cabbage and mustard sprouts add color to purées of rutabaga and carrot; smoked salmon mousse with sprouts; Gorgonzola-Stilton is piped over a cut piece of the same cheese.* Right: *Spears of Belgian endive filled with an orange-beet salad are arranged around the perimeter of a copper heart tray. The posy is made of grape hyacinths, bachelor buttons, and wood hyacinths.*

Sausage Roll Puffs

MAKES ABOUT
90 HORS D'OEUVRES

  1 *pound Puff Pastry
     (page 158)*
  1 *pound well-seasoned
     sausage meat*

Roll the puff pastry into a rectangle 15½ × 9 inches and cut the rectangle into three strips, each 3 inches wide.

Divide the sausage meat into thirds and roll each into a "snake" the length of the pastry. Place each roll of sausage along one edge of a pastry strip. Roll the pastry around the sausage and wet the edges with ice water and press to seal tightly. Chill the rolls for at least an hour.

Preheat the oven to 400°.

Cut the sausage rolls into ½-inch slices and put them on parchment-covered baking sheets. Bake until the pastry is puffed and golden brown, about 12 minutes. Serve warm, or reheat immediately before serving.

NOTE: The sausage rolls can be sliced and frozen before they are cooked. To bake, preheat the oven to 400° and cook the frozen puffs as above.

—»»› ‹‹‹«—

Fillet of Beef

MAKES APPROXIMATELY
40 HORS D'OEUVRES

HERB BUTTER
MAKES 1 CUP

  2 *tablespoons finely chopped
     parsley*

Another copper heart tray, garnished with a satin-tied bouquet of spring tulips, is piled high with light-as-a-feather sausage puffs.

. . . .

  1 *tablespoon finely chopped
     dill, chervil, or tarragon*
  1 *cup (2 sticks) unsalted
     butter, at room
     temperature*

  1 *2½- to 3-pound
     fillet of beef*
 ¼ *cup olive oil*
  4 *tablespoons coarsely
     ground black pepper*
  2 *loaves Homemade French
     Bread (page 159)
     Horseradish Cream
     (page 147)*

To make herb butter, chop the herbs in the bowl of a food processor, add softened butter, and mix together. Refrigerate until ready to use.

Trim all fat from the fillet. Rub the meat with olive oil and press the pepper into it.

Insert a spit through the length of the fillet, put it over a very hot fire, and cook by radiant heat until the meat is grilled to your taste. This will take anywhere from 15 to 30 minutes, depending on the size of the fillet and the intensity of the fire.

Transfer the meat to a board or platter, remove the spit, and carve into slices about ¼ inch thick. Serve on slices of French bread spread with herb butter and topped with a dollop of horseradish cream.

VARIATIONS: Use 1 pepper-and-oil-coated fillet that has been smoked in a commercial smoker or over mesquite smoke.

NOTE: Herb butter will keep up to 2 days in the refrigerator. To keep longer, freeze.

→»«←

Smoked Trout with Horseradish Cream

MAKES 30 TO 40 HORS D' OEUVRES

> 1   8-ounce smoked trout, filleted

HORSERADISH CREAM
MAKES 2 CUPS

> 1   cup heavy cream
> ¼   cup prepared horseradish, well drained

Separate filleted trout into chevrons, as shown. Arrange on a tray.

To make horseradish cream, whip the cream until stiff. Stir in the horseradish, mixing well. Spoon into a bowl and serve with the trout.

Radicchio with Wild Mushrooms and Parsley

MAKES 40 HORS D'OEUVRES

> 1   pound fresh wild mushrooms (chanterelles, pleurottes, shitake, porcini), cleaned
> 6   tablespoons olive oil
>   Salt and freshly ground black pepper to taste
> 6   tablespoons chopped fresh parsley
> ½   cup heavy cream
> 40 small radicchio leaves (about 6 small heads)

Cut the mushrooms into small pieces approximately ½ inch square. Sauté in olive oil for 2 to 3 minutes. Season with salt and pepper. Add the parsley and cream and bring to a simmer and remove from heat. Spoon onto small radicchio leaves and serve immediately.

· ·

Below left: *Fillet of beef with rosemary and watercress garnish.* Below right: *Chevrons of smoked trout.* Bottom: *Small leaves of radicchio can be used in many ways. We filled these with sautéed mushrooms. Another lettuce, Treviso, garnishes the tray with slices of star fruit.*

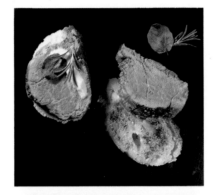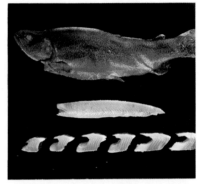

CHAPTER FOURTEEN

Master Recipes

T hroughout this book you will find that there are many hors d'oeuvres requiring pastry shells, puff pastry, blini, pancakes, pain de mie, French bread, and pâte à choux. I thought it best to group these recipes, many of which require special techniques, together in one chapter.

These are recipes that require skill and practice, and can be time-consuming, but they are worth the effort. Many pastry doughs can be made ahead, when one has time, and frozen until the day of the party. These master recipes should be learned by everyone, because they help not only in the creation of interesting hors d'oeuvres, but in other areas of cooking as well. For example, once you master the recipe for tartlet shells, you can make all kinds of savory and sweet pies and tarts for lunches, dinners, picnics, buffets, and other occasions.

. . . .

A variety of tartlets and tiny quiches—with an even greater variety of fillings—are made with the same basic pastry dough.

Tartlet Shells

MAKES 30 TO 40 SMALL,
1¹/₂- TO 2¹/₂-INCH TARTLETS

2 cups sifted flour
Pinch of salt
1¹/₂ sticks cold, unsalted butter
¹/₃ cup ice water

FILLING IDEAS

Eggplant, cut into small cubes, sautéed in olive oil with oregano
Chanterelles, sautéed in butter with tarragon
Zucchini, cut into small cubes, sautéed in olive oil with rosemary
Red pepper, cut into small pieces, sautéed in butter
Spinach, steamed and chopped
Zucchini, cut into small cubes, sautéed in butter with tarragon
Tomatoes, cut into small pieces, with sage
Sun-dried tomatoes, sliced, with slivers of mozzarella
Scallions, sautéed in butter, with cream cheese
Asparagus tips, steamed, with diced prosciutto or crabmeat
Shitake mushrooms, sautéed in butter with parsley
Artichoke hearts, sautéed in olive oil
Grated cheese and herbs

Combine flour and salt in the bowl of a food processor. Cut the butter into small pieces and add to the flour. Process quickly until the mixture resembles coarse meal. Add the water by droplets, mixing just until the dough holds together when pressed with your fingers; it should not be wet or sticky. Remove the dough from the bowl of the processor and press into a flat round, wrap in plastic wrap, and chill for 20 to 30 minutes.

To form the tartlets you will need twice as many tartlet pans as the quantity of shells you plan to make. Lightly butter or spray with vegetable oil the insides of half the pans.

Roll out half the pastry on a floured board into a round about ¹/₈ inch thick. Continually move the pastry around the board, turning over once or twice, to prevent sticking.

Put the tartlet pans on the pastry and, with a sharp knife, cut the pastry into pieces slightly larger than the pans. Place pastry in the prepared pans, pressing firmly, and cut off the excess pastry with your thumb. Press an unbuttered pan into each pastry-lined pan to act as a weight during baking. When all the pastry is used up, put the shells on a baking sheet and chill for at least 30 minutes.

Preheat the oven to 375°.

To bake the shells, set another baking sheet on top of the tartlets. (This will give additional weight and prevent puffing of the pastry.) Bake for 10 minutes, until the edges begin to color. Remove the top baking sheet and the liner pans, and continue to bake until the shells are lightly golden, about 5 to 7 additional minutes. Remove the shells from the pans and let cool on racks.

NOTE: If you will not be using the

Left: *Pastry dough can be rolled out and used to line tins of many shapes and sizes.* Right: *Puffs are made from a pâte à choux dough, which may be fried as well as baked, and varied by the addition of cheeses, herbs, or spices to the dough.*

• • • • • • • • • • • •

tartlet shells immediately, they can be cushioned with wax paper, stacked, and stored in an airtight container for up to 3 days.

Shells can also be frozen and re-crisped in a 350° oven; do not allow them to brown further.

VARIATION: To make 40 small, hors d'oeuvres-size quiches, whisk together 3 lightly beaten eggs, 1¹/₄ cups half-and-half or heavy cream, and salt and pepper to taste until smooth and well-combined. Pour a small amount of this custard into the baked tart shell over the desired filling and bake in a preheated 350° oven until the custard is set, about 8 minutes.

→≫《←

Pâte à Choux Puffs

MAKES ABOUT 40 PUFFS

1 cup water
8 tablespoons (1 stick) unsalted butter
¹/₄ teaspoon salt
¹/₂ teaspoon sugar
1 cup flour
4 large eggs

GLAZE

1 egg beaten with 1 teaspoon water

Put the water in a small, heavy saucepan. Cut the butter into small pieces and add to the water. Bring the water to a boil and melt the butter. Add the salt and sugar.

Remove from heat and add the flour. Stir until smooth.

Return to a high flame and continue stirring until the mixture forms a smooth mass, and the bottom of the pan is coated with a thin film. This indicates that the flour is cooked.

Remove from the stove and put the mixture in a mixing bowl. Let it cool slightly.

Add the eggs one at a time, beating the batter until very smooth.

Once the eggs have been added, the mixture can remain covered at room temperature for an hour or two.

Preheat the oven to 425°.

Pipe dough through a ½-inch pastry tube onto lightly buttered or parchment-covered baking sheets, forming mounds 1 inch in diameter and ¾ inch high. Lightly brush with the egg glaze, smoothing the top of each puff.

Bake for 10 minutes.

Reduce the temperature to 375° and continue baking until the puffs are golden brown, about 20 minutes. Reduce the oven to 325° and bake until the puffs are firm and the inside is not sticky or doughy.

Cool the puffs on a baking rack. They can be used immediately, or frozen in airtight containers. To use, warm in a preheated oven.

Rafael's Wild Rice Pancakes

MAKES 20 3-INCH PANCAKES

- ½   cup wild rice
- 1   cup water
- 2   tablespoons grated onion
- 4   tablespoons (½ stick) unsalted butter
- 1   cup flour
- 2   tablespoons baking powder
- 1   teaspoon salt
- 3   eggs, lightly beaten
- 1¼   cup milk
       Hot pepper jelly

In a saucepan, combine the rice and water. Bring to a boil, reduce heat, and simmer until rice is tender, 35 to 40 minutes. Drain well.

In a skillet, sauté onion in the butter until tender but not browned. Remove from the heat.

Sift the flour with the baking powder and salt.

In a medium mixing bowl, combine the onion, eggs, flour mixture, and milk, and stir until well blended. The batter should be smooth and slightly thicker than crêpe batter. If necessary, add more milk to reach the proper consistency. Stir in the wild rice.

Spoon 2 tablespoons of batter onto a hot, buttered skillet and cook until the pancakes are brown on one side; turn and cook about two min-

. . . .

Left: *Swedish pancakes are delicious with simple fillings of jellies and fresh berries. We have used apple jelly with red and black currants, quince jelly with red raspberries, currant jelly with blackberries, and slices of pear with whipped crème fraîche.* Right: *Special cast-iron pans with indentations make the creation of Swedish pancakes foolproof.*

utes longer. Serve hot with a dollop of hot pepper jelly.

VARIATIONS: Chop ½ pound wild or domestic mushrooms, sauté with the onions and add to batter.

Pancakes can be topped with whipped Crème Fraîche (page 60) and garnished with alfalfa sprouts.

→»«←

Swedish Pancakes

MAKES ABOUT 3 DOZEN

Swedish pancakes are made with an eggier, thinner, and slightly sweeter batter than that used for blini. Special cast-iron Swedish pancake pans are very useful—they are round with seven equal-size indentations to contain the batter during cooking.

- 3   eggs, slightly beaten
- 2   cups milk
- 1   cup all-purpose flour
- 6   tablespoons (¾ stick) melted unsalted butter
- ½   teaspoon salt
       Unsalted butter for the pan, melted

Combine the eggs, milk, flour, melted butter, and salt in a mixing bowl. Blend well.

Heat a Swedish pancake pan over medium heat. Spoon a small amount of butter in each indentation of the pan. When hot, pour 1 tablespoon of the batter in each section. Cook until puffed. Turn over and cook until golden brown, about 2 minutes. Put the pancakes on a heated platter in the oven and cover until ready to use.

To serve, put a dollop of the desired filling on one edge of the pancake and roll up.

FILLINGS AND TOPPINGS

Pears, whipped Crème Fraîche (page 60), and cinnamon
Pears, pear purée, and whipped cream cheese
Currant jelly and currants
Blackberry jelly and blackberries
Quince jelly and raspberries
Apple jelly and red currants
Black currant preserves and black currants

Blini

MAKES ABOUT 40 BLINI

We have discovered that small, individual blini, Swedish pancakes, and crêpes make excellent hors d'oeuvres. If well made, with light and tender batters, these members of the pancake family are interesting bases for an almost infinite number of toppings. The batters can be further enhanced by adding subtle amounts of herbs, flavored oils, wild rice, or different flours to the basic batters for more varied textures and flavors.

Necessary equipment varies, depending on which pancake you choose to make, but it is quite simple and generally inexpensive. Blini require a flat surface for cooking and a small spatula for turning. We use a flat, rectangular griddle for making blini in quantity, or a heavy skillet if we're making just a few. Hors d'oeuvre blini should be 2 to 3 inches in diameter.

1	**package of active dry yeast**
½	**cup warm water**
1	**cup milk**
1½	**cups all-purpose flour**
3	**eggs, separated**
½	**teaspoon salt** **Pinch of sugar**
6	**tablespoons (¾ stick) melted unsalted butter** **Additional butter for cooking**

Proof the yeast in warm water for 15 minutes.

Put the yeast mixture, milk, flour, egg yolks, salt, sugar, and melted butter in a blender or food processor. Blend at high speed for 40 seconds. Turn the machine off, scrape down the sides of the container, then blend for another few seconds. Pour the batter into a bowl that is large enough to accommodate the rising. Cover loosely and set in a warm place to rise for 1½ to 2 hours. Do not let batter rise much longer, or the blini will taste overfermented.

At cooking time, beat the egg whites until stiff. Fold them into the batter.

Heat a heavy skillet or griddle. Brush with melted butter. Drop batter by teaspoonful onto the hot pan. Turn the blini when the first side is lightly browned, and cook briefly on second side. Keep the blini on a heated platter until all the batter is used up.

→》《←

Buckwheat Blini

MAKES 75 COCKTAIL-SIZE BLINI

1	**package of active dry yeast**
1½	**cups warm water**
1½	**cups all-purpose flour**
1½	**cups buckwheat flour**
3	**eggs, separated**
4	**tablespoons (½ stick) melted unsalted butter** **Dash of salt**
1	**teaspoon sugar**
1½	**cups warm milk**

TOPPINGS

Sour cream and caviar
Melted butter and caviar

· · · · · · · · · · · ·

Left: **Blini are small yeast pancakes of Russian origin that can be cooked in a skillet, electric frying pan, or on a griddle, as shown here. Their flavor and texture can be altered by using white, whole-wheat, or buckwheat flour, or any combination of these.**

Sour cream and chives
or dill
Sour cream, caviar, and
chopped onions or
scallions
Additional butter for
cooking

Combine yeast and warm water in a medium bowl. Set in a warm place to proof for 15 to 20 minutes.

Slowly add the all-purpose flour to the yeast. Cover and let the dough rise for 1 hour.

Combine the buckwheat flour, egg yolks, butter, salt, sugar, and milk with the dough. Stir well to blend all the ingredients. Cover and let rise for 1 hour.

Just before cooking, beat the egg whites until stiff and fold them into the batter.

Heat a heavy skillet or griddle over a medium-high flame. Brush with butter. Drop 1 tablespoon of the batter into the hot pan. Cook until lightly browned, turn the blini, and cook briefly on the other side. Keep the blini on a heated platter until all the batter is used up.

To serve, put a dollop of the desired topping in the center of each blini.

VARIATIONS: Whole-wheat flour can be substituted for either the all-purpose or buckwheat flour.

→»«←

Crêpes

MAKES APPROXIMATELY 40
3-INCH OR 25 5-INCH CRÊPES

Crêpes can be made in large quantities on a flat rectangular electric or gas griddle. The batter should be poured onto the surface of the griddle with a one-quarter cup metal measuring cup; the flat bottom of the cup can be used to smooth the batter into a thin, round crêpe. A small, flexible metal spatula is best for turning the crêpes. French-iron crêpe pans come in many sizes, even a

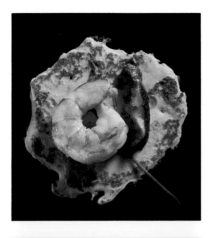

3-inch size, but we find it takes longer to make hors d'oeuvre crêpes in individual pans than on a flat griddle.

1¼	cups sifted all-purpose flour
4	eggs
1	cup milk
1¼	cups cold water
3	tablespoons unsalted butter, melted
½	teaspoon salt

In a blender or food processor, mix all ingredients at high speed for 30 seconds. Scrap down the sides and blend 30 seconds more. Pour batter into a mixing bowl and refrigerate for 1 hour.

Crêpes are ultra-thin pancakes that are perfect for topping with or wrapping around many foods. The crêpe batter itself can be enhanced with the addition of herbs. Top: A steamed shrimp and sautéed wild mushroom are served on a scallion crêpe. Center: A dill crêpe is wrapped around prosciutto and a spear of asparagus. Bottom: Folded cornucopia-style, these dill crêpes surround dill-garnished smoked salmon and whipped crème fraîche.

. . . .

To make 3-inch crêpes, spoon 2 tablespoons of batter into a hot, buttered crêpe pan (for 5-inch crêpes, use ¼ cup batter). Cook over medium-high heat until the surface is bubbly. Flip the crêpe and cook until golden brown, about 30 seconds. Remove from heat, and stack until ready to use.

NOTE: Crêpes can be made several hours before using and kept well wrapped at room temperature. To make them further in advance, freeze the wrapped crêpes and thaw in a microwave oven right before using.

VARIATIONS: To make dill crêpes, add 6 tablespoons finely chopped fresh dill to the blended batter and refrigerate. To make scallion crêpes, substitute 2 tablespoons melted unsalted butter and 1 tablespoon Oriental sesame oil for the 3 tablespoons butter, and add 6 tablespoons minced scallions to the blended batter. Refrigerate and cook as directed.

FILLINGS AND TOPPINGS

Smoked salmon, Crème
Fraîche (page 60), and fresh
dill
Sour cream and chives
Asparagus, prosciutto, and
hollandaise sauce
Sautéed shrimp and
shitake mushrooms

MASTER RECIPES

Phyllo Triangles

MAKES APPROXIMATELY
50 HORS D'OEUVRES

One-pound packages of paper-thin leaves are readily available in the freezers of most grocery stores.

1   pound phyllo pastry

FETA CHEESE AND SPINACH FILLING

1/3	cup olive oil
1	bunch scallions, chopped
2 1/2	pounds spinach, washed and dried (or 2 10-ounce packages frozen chopped spinach)
1	bunch parsley
1	bunch dill
1/2	pound feta cheese, drained and crumbled
3	eggs, lightly beaten
1	pound (4 sticks) unsalted butter

Thaw phyllo dough overnight in the refrigerator, if frozen.

To make the filling, heat the olive oil and sauté the scallions until soft. Add the spinach and cook until wilted, stirring frequently. Put the mixture in a colander over a bowl and press out the liquid.

In a small saucepan, boil down the spinach liquid until it measures 2 tablespoons. Add this back to the spinach mixture, along with the remaining filling ingredients and blend well. Season to taste and cool completely.

To assemble the triangles, melt and cool the butter. Place one sheet of phyllo on a flat surface and brush lightly with butter. Top this with two more sheets, buttering each. Cut the sheets in half lengthwise, then cut each half crosswise into 6 equal parts. Spoon a teaspoon of filling onto the end of each strip and form a triangle by folding the right-hand corner to the opposite side, as you would a flag. Continue folding until the entire strip is used.

Preheat oven to 400°.

Place triangles on a buttered baking sheet. Brush the tops of each with melted butter and bake until golden brown, about 10 minutes.

NOTE: Filled phyllo triangles can be kept in the refrigerator, unbaked, for 2 days, or frozen immediately for future use.

Filling Variations

CURRIED WALNUT CHICKEN FILLING

2	chicken breasts
2	tablespoons unsalted butter
2 1/2	tablespoons flour
1	teaspoon curry powder
1	cup milk
1/2	teaspoon salt
1/2	cup chopped walnuts

Bake chicken breasts in buttered aluminum foil for 45 minutes in a preheated 375° oven. Unwrap and cool. Remove skin and bones, and cut meat into small pieces.

Melt butter in a small pan, add flour and curry powder, and cook over low heat for 2 minutes. Add milk, whisk to blend, and continue to cook until thickened.

Season with salt, stir in walnuts and chicken, and cool completely before filling phyllo.

WILD MUSHROOM FILLING

5	tablespoons unsalted butter
1 1/2	pounds chanterelle or shitake mushrooms, coarsely chopped
1/2	cup Crème Fraîche (page 60)
3/4	cup chopped parsley Salt and pepper to taste Freshly ground nutmeg to taste

In a skillet, melt the butter over high heat, add the mushrooms and sauté for 2 to 3 minutes. Remove from heat and cool slightly.

Add the crème fraîche and chopped parsley to the mushrooms, and season to taste with salt, pepper, and nutmeg, and cool completely before filling phyllo.

LOBSTER FILLING

1	steamed lobster
4	tablespoons (1/2 stick) unsalted butter
6	scallions, finely chopped
1/4	cup white wine or vodka
1 1/2	tablespoons flour
1/4	cup heavy cream Pinch of cayenne pepper Salt and pepper to taste

Remove all the meat from the lobster and chop. Set aside.

Melt 2 tablespoons butter in a small skillet, and sauté the scallions for 2 or 3 minutes. Add the lobster meat and wine or vodka, and stir quickly to combine over high heat. Drain the mixture, reserving the liquid.

Melt the remaining 2 tablespoons butter in another skillet. Add the flour and cook slowly without coloring the flour for 5 minutes. Add the reserved liquid and the cream, and stir constantly until the mixture begins to thicken. Stir lobster meat back into mixture, add cayenne pepper, and season to taste. Cool mixture completely before filling phyllo.

· · · · · · · · · · · ·

Phyllo triangles are a very popular hors d'oeuvre. Many different fillings can be used (here, front to back: spinach and feta cheese, wild mushroom, and lobster fillings), but the technique for buttering and folding the triangle is standard. Hors d'oeuvres-size triangles are made with a portion of the phyllo sheet and a teaspoon of filling; entrée triangles are made with whole phyllo sheets and 3/4 cup filling.

Puff Pastry

MAKES APPROXIMATELY
5 POUNDS

- 2 **pounds all-purpose flour**
- 2 **pounds (8 sticks) unsalted butter**
- 2 **teaspoons salt**
- 2¼ **cups heavy cream**
  Additional flour for rolling

Weigh the flour accurately. In the bowl of a food processor or an electric mixer (using the flat paddle), or by hand, mix ¾ cup flour with the butter until smooth. Shape this mixture into a 1-inch-thick square, wrap well in plastic wrap, and chill for 30 minutes.

Combine the salt with the remaining flour and add the cream. With an electric mixer or by hand, beat well; the dough will not be completely smooth but it should not be sticky. Roll this dough out into a rectangle slightly wider than the square of butter/flour and twice as long. Center the square of butter on the dough, fold the dough to enclose butter completely, sealing the edges, and roll into a thick rectangle measuring 12 × 16 inches. Chill the rectangle for at least 30 minutes, so that the dough and butter are the same temperature.

Remove the dough from the refrigerator and roll out into a large rectangle ½ inch thick. Do not overwork the dough. Fold the dough into thirds, matching edges as carefully as possible and brushing off any excess flour. (It is important that the butter be distributed evenly between the layers of dough so that the pastry will puff evenly when baked.) Wrap the dough and chill for 30 minutes. This completes one "turn."

Repeat this process five more times (classic puff pastry gets six turns). Use as little flour as possible when rolling the dough out, and always brush off any excess before folding. By the sixth turn the dough should be very smooth, with no lumps of butter visible. Remember to let the dough rest in the refrigerator between turns; this can be speeded up by putting the dough in the freezer to chill.

Wrap the dough in plastic wrap and refrigerate until ready to use (up to 2 days). I often divide the dough into four or five pieces and freeze them individually wrapped, for future use.

Puff pastry squares can be topped with sesame or poppy seeds, or a small hollow made in the unbaked pastry for filling.

· · · · · · · · · · · ·

→》《←

Pain de Mie

MAKES 2 LOAVES

This basic French square loaf is especially excellent for hors d'oeuvres. Here is my adaptation of Julia Child's recipe from Mastering the Art of French Cooking, *Volume II.*

- 1 **2-ounce fresh cake yeast or 3 packages of active dry yeast**
- ½ **cup warm water**
- 5 **teaspoons salt**
- 4 **cups warm milk**
- 10 **cups unbleached white flour**
- 12 **tablespoons (1½ sticks) unsalted butter, at room temperature**

Dissolve the yeast in the warm water. Dissolve the salt in the warm milk. Be sure the temperature of the liquids does not exceed 100°, or the yeast may not proof.

Put the liquids in a large dough bowl, or in a large mixer with a dough hook. Add the flour, 2 to 3 cups at a time, mixing with a wooden spoon or dough hook until a sticky dough is formed. Turn out on a floured board, continuing to add flour and kneading until all 10 cups of flour have been incorporated and the dough is somewhat smooth. Add the butter, a tablespoon at a time, kneading until smooth. The dough will be lightly sticky.

Put the dough in a large bowl, cover with plastic wrap or a towel, and let it rise until almost tripled in bulk, about 2 to 3 hours. Punch down, knead for several minutes, and let rise a second time until doubled in bulk, about 1 more hour. Punch down and turn out on a floured board. Divide the dough in half (or two-thirds and one-third, depending upon the size of your pans). Flatten the dough into rectangle shapes the length of the pans; fold into thirds and put in two buttered pain de mie or 9 × 5 × 3-inch loaf pans. Press the dough carefully into the corners of the pans so air bubbles are broken. Cover the pans with sliding tops, if you are using traditional pain de mie pans, or with buttered cookie sheets and a heavy weight, and let rise until the dough fills two-thirds of the pan.

Preheat oven to 450°.

Bake for 30 to 40 minutes. Reduce the temperature to 375° and continue baking until the loaves are done, another 15 to 20 minutes. The bread should have risen to the

Soften the yeast in ¼ cup water.

Combine the flour and salt in a large mixing bowl. Add the remaining warm water and mix well. Add the yeast mixture and blend together.

Turn the dough out on a floured board and knead until it is smooth and elastic. (If you have a heavy-duty mixer with a dough hook, this whole procedure will take only 4 or 5 minutes.) Put the kneaded dough in a large bowl, cover, and let rise in a warm, draft-free place until doubled in bulk, about 1 hour. Punch the dough down and let rise a second time until doubled. Deflate again and turn out on a floured board.

To form baguettes, divide the dough into 6 equal pieces. Pat each into an oval, press down the middle of each with the edge of your hand, and fold the dough in half. Seal the edge with the heel of your hand, pressing hard to expel any air bubbles. Roll each oval into an even, cylindrical shape. Again, press down the middle with the edge of your hand, fold over, and seal edges and roll as if modeling clay.

Place baguettes into buttered pans. Cover lightly with plastic wrap and let rise until doubled in size. Uncover the loaves, and slash the top of each with a sharp razor blade, 3 or 4 cuts in each loaf.

Bake the baguettes in a preheated 400° oven until golden brown and crispy, about 25 minutes. To obtain a fine crust, spray the loaves with water three or four times during the baking.

VARIATIONS: To make whole-wheat French bread, use 3½ cups unbleached white flour and 3½ cups whole-wheat flour.

One cup raisins and/or ¾ cup walnut pieces can be added to the bread dough before the first rising.

Pain de mie is made with milk instead of water, a bit of sugar, and some butter. Baked in special, lidded rectangular pans, it makes a dense, firm, yet delicate bread that is easily sliced and cut with cookie cutters for hors d'oeuvres.

. . . .

tops of the pans, crusts should be golden brown, and sides slightly shrunk away from pan. When turned out, the loaves should sound hollow when tapped. If in doubt about doneness, return it to the oven and bake 5 to 10 minutes longer.

Turn out onto racks to cool, and wrap very well when cool. Pain de mie is best cut the second day. To keep it longer than 3 days, freeze well-wrapped bread.

To cut, slice with an electric slicer, if possible, or with a serrated bread knife, into slices ⅛ inch to ¼ inch thick.

→>>‹‹‹←

Homemade French Bread

MAKES 6 BAGUETTES

1	*1-ounce fresh cake yeast or 2 packages of active dry yeast*
2¾	*cups warm water*
7	*cups unbleached white flour*
4¼	*teaspoons salt*

Index

Page numbers in **boldface** refer to recipes.

A

Almond(s):
   spicy, *82*, **83**
   -stuffed dates with bacon, *122*, **125**

Anchovy filling, **31**

Antipasto party in the kitchen, *109–20*
   Brie en croûte, *110*, **118**
   crudité pickles, **116**
   eggplant slices sautéed in olive oil, *110*, **113**
   focaccia (Italian breads), *110*, **114**
   hard-boiled hen and quail eggs, *18*, **24**, *110*
   haricots verts, *110*, **113**
   marinated baby artichoke quarters, *110*, **111**
   marinated mushrooms, *110*, **113**
   marinated shrimp, *110*, **111**
   papaya, melon, or mango with prosciutto, *110*, **117**
   puff pastry straws, *70*, *110*, **114**
   roasted and marinated peppers, *110*, **111**
   Ruth Leserman's caramel Brie, *110*, **118**
   saucisson en croûte, *110*, **112**
   steamed red radishes, *110*, **113**
   Tuscan artichoke leaves, *110*, **117**

Apples with chicken liver pâté, *36*, **38–39**

Apricot(s):
   with bleu de Bresse, *36*, **45**
   dipping sauce, *82*, **85**

Artichoke(s):
   cherry tomatoes filled with hearts of palm and, **32**, *70*
   leaves, Tuscan, *110*, **117**
   quarters, marinated baby, *110*, **111**

Asparagus:
   crudités of haricots verts and, *70*, **71**
   pickled, **116**
   vinaigrette, *36*, **42**
   wrapped with prosciutto, *28*, **32**

B

Barbecue, outdoor, *47–56*
   barbecued beef strips, *48*, **50**
   barbecued chicken wings, *48*, **54–55**
   blackened leeks, *48*, **49**
   chicken and pepper skewers, *48*, **52–53**
   chicken wing "legs," *48*, **53**
   cocktail ribs, *48*, **54**
   fresh fruit daiquiris, *48*, **55**
   grilled eggplant, *48*, **50**
   grilled sausages, *48*, **55**
   lamb and eggplant skewers, *48*, **52**
   piña coladas, *48*, **55**
   pork and mango skewers, *48*, **53**
   skewered okra, *48*, **49**
   veal and pearl onion skewers, *48*, **52**

Bar equipment, **9**

Barquettes with leek chiffonade, *70*, **76**

Bean burritos, *128*, **134–35**

Beef:
   chili, corn cups filled with, *128*, **132**
   fillet of, *140*, **146–47**
   strips, barbecued, *48*, **50**

Beets:
   endive with mustard sprouts and, *140*, **144**
   yellow pickled, **116**

Beignets with powdered sugar, *122*, **123**

Biscuits with whipped crème fraîche, *18*, **23**

Black bean(s):
   sauce, **98–99**
   spicy, **134–35**

Blackberry butter, heart scones with, *58*, **66**

Bleu de Bresse:
   apricots with, *36*, **45**
   topping, **72**

Blini, **154**
   buckwheat, **154–55**
   with sour cream and caviar, *102*, **105**
   bloody Marys, *122*, **125**

Bread, French, *see* French bread

Breads, Italian (focaccia), *110*, **114**

Breakfast buffet, *121–26*
   almond-stuffed dates with bacon, *122*, **125**
   beignets with powdered sugar, *122*, **123**
   bloody Marys, *122*, **125**
   corn muffins with smoked turkey, *122*, **124**
   crêpes with cinnamon pears, *122*, **123**
   French toast triangles with maple butter, *122*, **123**
   Mary's knees, *122*, **125**
   orange muffins with smoked duck breast, *122*, **124**
   tartlet shells filled with scrambled eggs, *122*, **123**
   zucchini fritters, *122*, **125**

Brie:
   en croûte, *110*, **118**
   Ruth Leserman's caramel, *110*, **118**

Brine, pickling, **24**

Brioche dough, **112**

Buckwheat blini, **154–55**

Burritos, bean, *128*, **134–5**

Butter:
   blackberry, *58*, **66**
   coriander, **50**
   herb, **146–47**
   lemon, **106**
   lime, **107**
   magenta, **106**
   maple, *122*, **123**
   orange, **106**
   sage, **49**
   thyme, **49**

C

Cardinales, *28*, **32**

Carpaccio on French bread, *102*, **103**

Carrots, pickled, **116**

Cauliflower balls, **135**

Caviar:
   black and red, heart toasts with, *102*, **103**
   blini with sour cream and, *102*, **105**
   golden, clams with Italian parsley and, *102*, **105**
   red potatoes with sour cream and, *140*, **142**
   salmon roe, heart-shaped toast with, *58*, **60**
   Sevruga, oysters with, *102*, **106–7**

Caviar, eggplant, on French bread toast, *58*, **63**

Chanterelle topping, **60**

Cheese:
    chili peppers and, *133*
    croque monsieur, *36*, **37**
    herb, *72*, **143**
    red pepper, pattypan squash filled
        with, *28*, **29**
    see also specific cheeses

Chicken:
    pecan salad, **73**
    and pepper skewers, *48*, **52–53**
    salad tartlets, Oriental, *70*, **74**
    skewers, *140*, **141**
    sugar-tea smoked, *82*, **88–89**
    and veal pâté, *36*, **41**
    walnut filling, curried, **156**
    wing ''legs,'' *48*, **53**
    wings, barbecued, *48*, **54–55**

Chicken liver pâté, apples with, *36*,
    38–39

Chili:
    beef, corn cups filled with, *128*, **132**
    green, *133*

Chili peppers and cheese, **133**

Chinese pearl balls, *82*, **83**

Chocolate cookies, broken heart, *58*,
    66–67

Chorizo and scrambled eggs, **133**

Christmas, *see* Cocktails, Christmas

Cilantro sauce, **98**

Cinnamon pears, crêpes with, *122*, **123**

Clams:
    with golden caviar and Italian
        parsley, *102*, **105**
    grilled, with barbecue sauce, *92*,
        98–99

Cocktails, Christmas, *27–33*
    asparagus wrapped with prosciutto,
        28, **32**
    baked oysters red and green, *28*, **30**
    cardinales, *28*, **32**
    cherry tomatoes filled with smoked
        salmon mousse, *28*, **30–32**
    pattypan squash filled with red
        pepper cheese, *28*, **29**
    savory wreath, *28*, **30**
    skewered tortellini with roasted
        garlic garnish, *28*, **29**, *140*, **141**

Cocktails, fancy, *139–48*
    chicken skewers, *140*, **141**
    endive with beets and mustard
        sprouts, *140*, **144**
    fillet of beef, *140*, **146–47**
    radicchio with wild mushrooms and
        parsley, *140*, **147**
    red potatoes with sour cream and
        caviar, *140*, **142**

sausage roll puffs, *140*, **146**
shrimp wrapped in snow peas, *140*,
    142
skewered tortellini, *140*, **141**
smoked trout with horseradish
    cream, *140*, **147**
snow peas with crabmeat filling,
    140, **143**

Cocktails, Oriental, *81–90*
    apricot dipping sauce, *82*, **85**
    baby ribs, *82*, **87**
    Chinese pearl balls, *82*, **83**
    garlic-soy dipping sauce, *82*, **85**
    mangoes, *82*, **89**
    minted melon balls, *82*, **89**
    plum sauce, *82*, **85**
    shrimp toast, *82*, **87**
    spicy almonds, *82*, **83**
    steamed dumplings, *82*, **86**
    sugar-tea smoked chicken, *82*,
        88–89
    tea smoked eggs with sesame salt,
        82, **84**
    tea smoked shrimp, *82*, **88**
    wontons, *82*, **85**

Coeur à la crème with cucumber
    hearts, *58*, **59**

Containers, *8*

Cookie(s):
    broken heart chocolate, *58*, **66–67**
    gingerbread cupids, *58*, **67**
    hearts, sugar, *58*, **67**

Coriander butter, **50**

Corn:
    cups filled with beef chili, *128*,
        132–33
    salad, **32**
    tortillas, **135**

Corn muffins with smoked turkey, *122*,
    124

Country kitchen hors d'oeuvres, *34–46*
    apples with chicken liver pâté, *36*,
        38–39
    apricots with bleu de Bresse, *36*, **45**
    asparagus vinaigrette, *36*, **42**
    baked red potatoes with toppings,
        36, *140*, **142**
    chicken and veal pâté, *36*, **41**
    country pâté, *36*, **41**
    croque monsieur, *36*, **37**
    duck pâté, *36*, **39**
    duck rillettes, *36*, **37**
    frittatas, *36*, **42**
    galantine of duck, *36*, **42**
    homemade French bread, *36*, *41*,
        159
    tiny pizzas, *36*, **45**

Crab(s):

claws, stone, with four-pepper
    sauce, *92*, **99**
Dungeness, with herb mayonnaise,
    92, **96**

Crabmeat:
    empanaditas, fresh, *128*, **136**
    filling, snow peas with, *140*, **143**
    salad, **72–73**

Cream puffs with jam and powdered
    sugar, *18*, **23**

Crème fraîche, **60**
    whipped, biscuits with, *18*, **23**

Crêpes, **155**
    with cinnamon pears, *122*, **123**
    pear-filled, *70*, **79**

Croque monsieur, *36*, **37**

Crudité pickles, **116**

Crudités of asparagus and haricots
    verts, *70*, **71**

Cucumber:
    hearts, coeur à la crème with, *58*, **59**
    rounds with smoked salmon
        mousse, *70*, **72–73**

Currant(s):
    chicken liver pâté with, **38**
    sauce, grilled boned quail with, *58*,
        62–63

Cutting tools, *8*

D · · · · · · · · · ·

Daiquiris, fresh fruit, *48*, **55**

Dates, almond-stuffed, with bacon,
    122, **125**

Decorative equipment, *9*

Deviled eggs, *18*, **24**

Dip:
    lemon, **71**
    Parmesan lemon, **141**

Dipping sauce:
    apricot, *82*, **85**
    chicken and pepper skewer, **52–53**
    garlic-soy, *82*, **85**
    steamed dumpling, **86**
    tuna sashimi, **105**

Drinks:
    Bloody Marys, *122*, **125**
    cardinales, *28*, **32**
    fresh fruit daiquiris, *48*, **55**
    margaritas, **136–37**
    Mary's knees, *122*, **125**
    piña coladas, *48*, **55**

sparkling kirs, *58*, **67**

Duck:
    breast, smoked, orange muffins
        with, *122*, **124**
    galantine of, *36*, **42**
    pâté, *36*, **39**
    rillettes, *36*, **37**

Dumplings, steamed, *82*, **86**

E

Eggplant:
    caviar on French bread toast, *58*, **63**
    grilled, *48*, **50**
    and lamb skewers, *48*, **52**
    slices sautéed in olive oil, *110*, **113**

Eggs:
    deviled, *18*, **24**
    glaze, **136**
    hard-boiled, **24**, *110*
    scrambled, chorizo and, **133**
    scrambled, tartlet shells filled with,
        122, **123**
    tea smoked, with sesame salt, *82*, **84**
    see also Quail eggs

Empanaditas, fresh crab, *128*, **136**

Endive with beets and mustard sprouts,
    140, **144**

Equipment and tools, *8–9*

Escabèche, *92*, **94–95**

F

Feta cheese and spinach filling, **156**

Fillings:
    burrito, **134–35**
    cherry tomato, **30–32**
    corn cup, **132–33**
    crêpe, **155**
    empanadita, **136**
    endive, **144**
    phyllo triangle, **156**
    red pepper cheese, **29**
    snow pea, **143**
    steamed dumpling, **86**
    Swedish pancake, **153**
    tartlet shell, **74**, **150**

Fish escabèche, *92*, **94**

Focaccia (Italian breads), *110*, **114**

Foie gras with Black Forest mushrooms
    on French bread toast, *58*, **60**,
    102

French bread:
    carpaccio on, *102*, **103**
    eggplant caviar on, *58*, **63**
    foie gras with Black Forest
        mushrooms on, **60**, *102*
    homemade, *36*, **159**

French toast triangles with maple
    butter, *122*, **123**

Frittatas, *36*, **42**

Fritters, zucchini, *122*, **125**

Fruit, *see specific fruits*

G

Galantine of duck, *36*, **42**

Garlic:
    garnish, roasted, skewered tortellini
        with, *28*, **29**
    -soy dipping sauce, *82*, **85**

Gingerbread cupids, *58*, **67**

Gorditas, *128*, **135**

Gorgonzola cheese, pears with, *70*, **73**

Gorgonzola-Stilton cheese filling, **144**

Goujonettes of sole, *92*, **95**

Grand and elegant party, *101–8*
    blini with sour cream and caviar,
        102, **105**
    carpaccio on French bread, *102*, **103**
    clams with golden caviar and Italian
        parsley, *102*, **105**
    foie gras with Black Forest
        mushrooms on French bread
        toast, *58*, **60**, *102*
    heart toasts with black and red
        caviar, *102*, **103**
    oysters with Sevruga caviar, *102*,
        106–7
    tuna sashimi with black seaweed,
        102, **105**

Grapes, Roquefort, *70*, **78**

Gravlax with fennel, *58*, **64–65**

Guacamole, *128*, **129**

H

Haricots verts, *110*, **113**
    crudités of asparagus and, *70*, **71**

Hors d'oeuvre parties, *1–15*
    crudité parties vs., *11*
    decorations, garnishes, and
        arrangements for, *7*, *11–14*

hearty, *3*, *10*
    kinds of food for, *3*
    light, *3*, *10*
    trays for, *9*, *14*
    types of, *10–15*
    unusual glassware for, *14–15*
    variations for, *6–7*
    see also specific occasions

Horseradish cream, smoked trout with,
    140, **147**

I

Italian breads (focaccia), *110*, **114**

K

Kirs, sparkling, *58*, **67**

Kitchen equipment, *9*

L

Lamb and eggplant skewers, *48*, **52**

Lamb chops, baby, with mint sauce, *58*,
    63

Leek(s):
    blackened, *48*, **49**
    chiffonade, barquettes with, *70*, **76**

Lemon:
    butter, **106**
    dip, **71**
    Parmesan dip, **141**

Lime butter, **107**

Lobster filling, **156**

M

Mango(es), *82*, **89**
    papaya or melon with prosciutto,
        110, **117**
    and pork skewers, *48*, **53**

Maple butter, French toast triangles
    with, *122*, **123**

Margaritas, *128*, **136–37**

Marinade:
    Oriental baby ribs, **87**
    shrimp, **142**
    smoked duck, **124**

Mary's knees, *122*, **125**

Mayonnaise:
  herb, *92*, **96**
  homemade, **20**

Meat, *see specific meats*

Melon:
  balls, minted, *82*, **89**
  papaya or mango with prosciutto, *110*, **117**

Mint sauce, baby lamb chops with, *58*, **63**

Mousse:
  smoked salmon, cherry tomatoes filled with, *28*, **30–31**
  smoked salmon, cucumber rounds with, *70*, **72–73**
  smoked trout, **73**

Mozzarella and olive oil, **32**

Muffins:
  corn, with smoked turkey, *122*, **124**
  orange, with smoked duck breast, *122*, **124**
  orange, with smoked turkey, *70*, **76–77**

Mushroom(s), wild:
  filling, **156**
  radicchio with parsley and, *140*, **147**

Mushrooms:
  Black Forest, on French bread toast, foie gras with, **60**, *102*
  marinated, *110*, **113**

Mussels, steamed green, *92*, **96**

Mustard:
  sauce, **64–65**
  vinaigrette, creamy grainy, **113**

Mustard sprouts, endive with beets and, *140*, **144**

N

Nachos, *128*, **130**

Nuts, *see specific nuts*

O

Okra:
  pickled, **116**
  skewered, *48*, **49**

Onion, pearl, and veal skewers, *48*, **52**

Onions, curried, puffs with, *70*, **76**

Orange:
  butter, **106**

muffins with smoked duck breast, *122*, **124**
muffins with smoked turkey, *70*, **76—77**

Oriental baby ribs, *82*, **87**

Oriental chicken salad tartlets, *70*, **74**

Oriental cocktails, *see* Cocktails, Oriental

Oysters:
  red and green, baked, *28*, **30**
  with Sevruga caviar, *102*, **106–7**

P

Pain de mie, **158–59**

Palm, hearts of, cherry tomatoes filled with artichokes and, **32**, *70*

Pancakes:
  Rafael's wild rice, **153**
  Swedish, **153**

Pans, *8*

Papaya, melon, or mango with prosciutto, *110*, **117**

Parmesan lemon dip, **141**

Pasta, pesto, **32**

Pâté:
  apples with chicken liver, *36*, **38–39**
  chicken and veal, *36*, **41**
  country, *36*, **41**
  duck, *36*, **39**

Pâté à choux puffs, **150**

Pattypan squash filled with red pepper cheese, *28*, **29**

Pear(s):
  cinnamon, crêpes with, *122*, **123**
  -filled crêpes, *70*, **79**
  with Gorgonzola, *70*, **73**

Pecan chicken salad, **73**

Peppers, bell:
  and chicken skewers, *48*, **52–53**
  red, tomato sauce, **98**
  roasted and marinated, *110*, **111**
  sauce, four-, stone crab claws with, *92*, **99**
  and shrimp tortillas, *128*, **136**
  yellow pickled, **116**

Pesto pasta, **32**

Phyllo triangles, **156**

Pickled quail eggs, *18*, **24**

Pickled vegetables, crudité, **116**

Pico de gallo sauce, *128*, **130**

Piña coladas, *48*, **55**

Pizzas, tiny, *36*, **45**

Plum sauce, *82*, **85**

Pork:
  cocktail ribs, *48*, **54**
  and mango skewers, *48*, **53**
  Oriental baby ribs, *82*, **87**
  ribs, cocktail, *48*, **54**

Pork sausage (chorizo) and scrambled eggs, **133**

Potatoes, baked red, with sour cream and caviar, *36*, *140*, **142**

Poultry, *see specific poultry*

Preserves, pear, **79**

Prosciutto:
  asparagus wrapped with, *28*, **32**
  papaya, melon, or mango with, *110*, **117**

Puff pastry, **158**
  straws, *70*, *110*, **114**

Purée, vegetable, **144**

Q

Quail, grilled boned, with currant sauce, *58*, **62–63**

Quail eggs:
  pickled, *18*, **24**
  with seasoned salt, hard-boiled, *18*, **24**, *110*

Quesadillas, *128*, **131**

R

Radicchio with wild mushrooms and parsley, *140*, **147**

Radishes:
  pickled, **116**
  steamed red, *110*, **113**

Rafael's wild rice pancakes, **153**

Recipes, master, **149–59**
  blini, **154**
  buckwheat blini, **154–55**
  crêpes, **155**
  homemade French bread, **159**
  pain de mie, **158–59**
  pâté à choux puffs, **150–51**
  phyllo triangles, **156**

puff pastry, *158*
Rafael's wild rice pancakes, *153*
Swedish pancakes, *153*
tartlet shells, *150*

Red pepper cheese, pattypan squash filled with, *28*, *29*

Ribs:
cocktail, *48*, **54**
Oriental baby, *82*, **87**

Rice, in Chinese pearl balls, *82*, **83**

Rice, wild, pancakes, Rafael's, *153*

Rillettes, duck, *36*, **37**

Roquefort grapes, *70*, **78**

Ruth Leserman's caramel brie, *110*, **118**

S

Sage butter, **49**

Salad:
corn, **32**
crabmeat, **72–73**
curried tuna, **73**
Oriental chicken, tartlets, *70*, **74**
pecan chicken, **73**

Salmon:
grilled, with thyme, *92*, **93**
mousse, smoked, cherry tomatoes filled with, *28*, **30–31**
mousse, smoked, cucumber rounds with, *70*, **72–73**

Salmon roe caviar, heart-shaped toast with, *58*, **60**

Salsa roja, *128*, **129**

Salt, seasoned, *18*, **24**

Sandwiches:
ham-and-cheese, **37**
tea, *18*, **19**

Sashimi, tuna, with black seaweed, *102*, **105**

Sauce:
apricot dipping, *82*, **85**
barbecue, *92*, **98**
black bean, **98–99**
carpaccio, **103**
cilantro, **98**
currant, *58*, **62–63**
dipping, **52–53**
four-pepper, *92*, **99**
garlic-soy dipping, *82*, **85**
mint, *58*, **63**
mustard, **64–65**
pico de gallo, *128*, **130**

plum, *82*, **85**
salsa roja, *128*, **129**
tartar, **95**
tomatillo, *128*, **129**
tomato red pepper, **98**
see also Dipping sauce

Saucisson en croûte, *110*, **112**

Sausage(s):
grilled, *48*, **55**
pork (chorizo), and scrambled eggs, **133**
roll puffs, *140*, **146**
saucisson en croûte, *110*, **112**

Savories, herb, *18*, **20**

Savory wreath, *28*, **30**

Scallops:
grilled, with chervil and fennel, *92*, **93**
seviche of, *128*, **134**

Scones:
heart, with blackberry butter, *58*, **66**
with herb jellies, *18*, **22**

Seafood, *91–100*
Dungeness crabs with herb mayonnaise, *92*, **96**
escabèche, *92*, **94–95**
goujonettes of sole, *92*, **95**
grilled clams with barbecue sauce, *92*, **98–99**
grilled salmon with thyme, *92*, **93**
grilled scallops with chervil and fennel, *92*, **93**
grilled swordfish with cherry tomatoes and fennel leaves, *92*, **93**
grilled tiger shrimp with dill, *92*, **93**
grilled tuna with black pepper, *92*, **94**
herb mayonnaise, *92*, **96**
steamed green mussels, *92*, **96**
stone crab claws with four-pepper sauce, *92*, **99**
see also specific seafood

Seaweed, black, tuna sashimi with, *102*, **105**

Serving pieces, *9*

Sesame salt, tea smoked eggs with, *82*, **84**

Seviche of scallops, *128*, **134**

Shortbread flavored with cayenne, heart-shaped, *18*, **20**

Shrimp:
grilled, wrapped in bacon, *58*, **64**
grilled tiger, with dill, *92*, **93**
marinade, **142**

marinated, *110*, **111**
and pepper tortillas, *128*, **136**
tea smoked, *82*, **88**
toast, *82*, **87**
wrapped in snow peas, *140*, **142**

Slicing tools, *8*

Snow peas:
with crabmeat filling, *140*, **143**
shrimp wrapped in, *140*, **142**

Sole, goujonettes of, *92*, **95**

Soy-garlic dipping sauce, *82*, **85**

Spinach filling, feta cheese and, **156**

Squash, pattypan, filled with red pepper cheese, *28*, **29**

Squash, yellow pickled, **116**

Steak tartare, **31**

String beans, pickled, **116**

Swedish pancakes, *153*

Swordfish, grilled, with cherry tomatoes and fennel leaves, *92*, **93**

T

Tacos la salsa, *128*, **130–31**

Tartar sauce, **95**

Tartlet shells, *150*
filled with scrambled eggs, *122*, **123**

Tartlets, Oriental chicken salad, *70*, **74**

Tea:
smoked chicken, sugar-, *82*, **88–89**
smoked eggs with sesame salt, *82*, **84**
smoked shrimp, *82*, **88**

Tea party, *17–26*
biscuits with whipped crème fraîche, *18*, **23**
cream puffs with jam and powdered sugar, *18*, **23**
deviled eggs, *18*, **24**
hard-boiled quail eggs with seasoned salt, *18*, **24**
heart-shaped shortbread flavored with cayenne, *18*, **20**
herb mayonnaise, *92*, **96**
herb savories, *18*, **20**
homemade mayonnaise, **20**
pickled quail eggs, *18*, **24**
scones with herb jellies, *18*, **22**
tea sandwiches, *18*, **19**

Tea sandwiches, *18*, **19**

Tex-Mex hors d'oeuvres, *127–38*
   bean burritos, *128*, **134–35**
   corn cups filled with beef chili, *128*, **132–33**
   fresh crab empanaditas, *128*, **136**
   gorditas, *128*, **135**
   guacamole, *128*, **129**
   margaritas, *128*, **136–37**
   nachos, *128*, **130**
   pico de gallo sauce, *128*, **130**
   quesadillas, *128*, **131**
   salsa roja, *128*, **129**
   seviche of scallops, *128*, **134**
   shrimp and pepper tortillas, *128*, **136**
   tacos la salsa, *128*, **130–31**
   tomatillo sauce, *128*, **129**
   tortas de coliflor, *128*, **135**
   tortilla chips, *128*, **129**

Thyme butter, **49**

Tomatillo sauce, *128*, **129**

Tomato(es):
   pico de gallo sauce, *128*, **130**
   red pepper sauce, **98**
   salsa roja, *128*, **129**

Tomatoes, cherry:
   filled with hearts of palm and, *32*, *70*
   filled with smoked salmon mousse, *28*, **30–32**
   grilled swordfish with fennel leaves and, *92*, **93**

Tomatoes, sundried, mozzarella, and olive oil, **32**

Toppings:
   blini, **154–55**
   crêpe, **155**
   cucumber round, **72–73**
   focaccia, **114**
   foie gras, **60**
   grilled clam, **98–99**
   oysters with Sevruga caviar, **106–7**
   red potato, **142**
   Swedish pancake, **153**
   tea sandwich, **19**

tiny pizza, **45**

Tortas de coliflor, *128*, **135**

Tortellini, skewered, with roasted garlic garnish, *28*, **29**, **140**, **141**

Tortilla chips, *128*, **129**

Tortillas:
   corn, **135**
   shrimp and pepper, *128*, **136**

Trays, *9*, *14*

Trout, smoked:
   with horseradish cream, *140*, **147**
   mousse, **73**

Tuna:
   grilled, with black pepper, *92*, **94**
   salad, curried, **73**
   sashimi with black seaweed, *102*, **105**

Turkey, smoked:
   corn muffins with, *122*, **124**
   orange muffins with, *70*, **76–77**

Turnips, pickled, **116**

V

Valentine's Day, *57–69*
   baby lamb chops with mint sauce, *58*, **63**
   broken heart chocolate cookies, *58*, **66–67**
   coeur à la crème with cucumber hearts, *58*, **59**
   crème fraîche, **60**
   eggplant caviar on French bread toast, *58*, **63**
   gingerbread cupids, *58*, **67**
   gravlax with fennel, *58*, **64–65**
   grilled boned quail with currant sauce, *58*, **62–63**
   grilled shrimp wrapped in bacon, *58*, **64**
   heart scones with blackberry butter, *58*, **66**
   heart-shaped toast with salmon roe

caviar, *58*, **60**
   sautéed foie gras, *58*, **60**
   sparkling kirs, *58*, **67**
   sugar cookie hearts, *58*, **67**

Veal:
   and chicken pâté, *36*, **41**
   and pearl onion skewers, *48*, **52**

Vegetables:
   crudité pickled, **116**
   purée, **144**
   savory wreath, *28*, **30**
   see also specific vegetables

Vinaigrette:
   asparagus, *36*, **42**
   creamy grainy mustard, **113**

W

Walnut chicken filling, curried, **156**

Wedding reception, *10–11*, *69–80*
   barquettes with leek chiffonade, *70*, **76**
   cherry tomatoes filled with artichokes and hearts of palm, **32**, *70*, *74*
   crudités of asparagus and haricots verts, *70*, **71**
   cucumber rounds with smoked salmon mousse, *70*, **72–73**
   orange muffins with smoked turkey, *70*, **76–77**
   Oriental chicken salad tartlets, *70*, **74**
   pear-filled crêpes, *70*, **79**
   pears with Gorgonzola, *70*, **73**
   puff pastry straws, *70*, *110*, **114**
   puffs with curried onions, *70*, **76**
   Roquefort grapes, *70*, **78**

Wontons, *82*, **85**

Z

Zucchini fritters, *122*, **125**